THE CHAPLAINS AT HALE SCOUT RESERVATION

COMPILED BY DAVID COX

USA • Canada • UK • Ireland

All Scripture is from the Life Application Study Bible of the New Living Translation unless specified differently.

© Copyright 2006 David Cox (dcox@tulsacoxmail.com).
All rights reserved. No part of this publication may be reproduced, stored in a retrieval system, or transmitted, in any form or by any means, electronic, mechanical, photocopying, recording, or otherwise, without the written prior permission of the author.

Note for Librarians: A cataloguing record for this book is available from Library and Archives Canada at www.collectionscanada.ca/amicus/index-e.html
ISBN 1-4120-9310-4

Printed in Victoria, BC, Canada. Printed on paper with minimum 30% recycled fibre. Trafford's print shop runs on "green energy" from solar, wind and other environmentally-friendly power sources.

Offices in Canada, USA, Ireland and UK

Book sales for North America and international:
Trafford Publishing, 6E–2333 Government St.,
Victoria, BC V8T 4P4 CANADA
phone 250 383 6864 (toll-free 1 888 232 4444)
fax 250 383 6804; email to orders@trafford.com

Book sales in Europe:
Trafford Publishing (UK) Limited, 9 Park End Street, 2nd Floor
Oxford, UK OX1 1HH UNITED KINGDOM
phone +44 (0)1865 722 113 (local rate 0845 230 9601)
facsimile +44 (0)1865 722 868; info.uk@trafford.com

Order online at:
trafford.com/06-1064

10 9 8 7 6 5 4 3

Camp Tom Hale is a Boy Scout Camp nestled in the scenic Quachita National Forest in Southeastern Oklahoma. Since 1961 it has welcomed Scouts of all ages offering them outdoor activities of Astronomy, canoeing, kayaking, sailboating, climbing, snow skiing, and horsemanship among 40 other challenging merit badge programs.

Chapel Services have always been an integral part of the camping experience, but they would ebb and flow, dependent upon if, and who, the camp was able to recruit to be chaplain for the six to eight week summer commitment. In the mid-nineties the camp was experiencing a declining chapel service. Then, a Baptist minister took the initiative to rebuild the program. This is the story of how this new program changed a daily attendance at chapel from a handful of scouts to an attendance that sometimes has as many as 400 scouts and leaders.

Learn here how the program was turned around and read about some of the short devotions that bring the scouts and leaders back bright and early each and every day of the week long camping experience. You will find these devotions not only exciting reading, but also helpful in using or creating your own devotions for Sunday School classes, Children's sermons, and other religious group gatherings.

Contents

Dedication 6

Foreword 7

Chapter One: A Short History of Scouting 9

Chapter Two: Hale Scout Reservation 19

Chapter Three: Chaplain Layman David Cox Opening Comments 21

Chapter Four: Introduction to Devotions 23

Chapter Five: Favorite Devotions 27

Chapter Six: Devotion Ideas And Helpful Suggestions From Other
    HSR Chaplains 89

Chapter Seven: Compilation Of Helpful Ideas And Sources Of Handouts . . 93

Chapter Eight: Pick Your Music 99

Conclusion 149

Dedication

This book is dedicated to our Almighty God who by His Creations has made scouting and camping an experience that is unequaled by any other activity a young person may become involved in. Colossians 1: 16- 17

> *16/ "For by Him all things were created; everything in heaven and earth. He made the things we can see and the things we can't see...17/ He existed before everything else began, and he holds all creation together."*

Half of the proceeds from this book will be shared evenly between the Indian Nation Council of Scouting in Oklahoma and the National Headquarters of BSA.

FOREWORD

This book is in remembrance of two young Eagle Scouts, Joel Martin and Tyler Moody, who because of separate untimely accidents are no longer with us but are with their Father in Heaven. God used them to embolden and encourage me to reach out to Scouts not just in one troop or one Council but worldwide and help them recognize God as the ruling and leading power in the universe. This book is to serve as a tool to help others to touch the lives of young men and women, helping them to become the moral leaders of our civilization and the builders of worldwide peace.

CHAPTER ONE

A SHORT HISTORY OF SCOUTING

Scouting is a worldwide organization that not only teaches boys and girls to be good citizens but to be helpful and self reliant. Membership has no racial or religious barriers. Worldwide there are over 28 million Boy Scouts and Scout Leaders while the Girl Scouts can boast over 2.5 million members and adult leaders. United States membership of BSA (Boy Scouts of America) is nearly 6 million strong.

There are over 130,000 units (Packs, Troops, and Posts) organized in some 400 local councils in BSA.

The Boy Scout movement was founded in England by Robert S.S. Baden-Powell in 1908. It appealed to boys because of its adventure and outdoor activities, and helped mold good citizenship. In 1909, William Boyce, a Chicago Publisher, learned about the movement while he was visiting in London. Through his leadership, BSA was founded on February 8, 1910. After this it began to spread rapidly around the world.

Information from the Boy Scouts of America (BSA) headquarters in Irving, Texas, www.bsamuseum.org, tells us that at the end of 2004 there were over 6.2 million youth and leaders who were members of BSA.

The World Organization of the Scout Movement (WOSM) began in 1922. Their International Headquarters are also in Irving, Texas, next to the BSA Headquarters. Their website, www.scout.org, shows that worldwide membership in scouting as of 2004 was more than 28 million. Of this, there are 17 million (or 68%) in the Asian Pacific Region. World Scouting is divided up into six regions: Asian Pacific, Arab, African, European, Eurasia, and Inter-America.

The Asian-Pacific Region which has the largest number of Scouts, consists of 25 countries and territories. There are only 6 countries where Scouting is not allowed or does not exist.

Although each country may have some differences in their programs, they all adhere to the 10 fundamental principals. And the first of which is a duty to God and a respect for individual beliefs.

The countries with the largest number of Scouts and the percentage of Scouts as compared to that countries population are as follows:

Country	Number in Scouting	% as of Total Population
Indonesia	8,909,435	3.7%
United States	6,239,435	2.1%
Philippines	1,956,131	2.2%
Thailand	1,305,027	2.1%

When one looks at a countries principal religion, one can surmise that approximately 1/3rd of today's scouts are Muslim. Another 1/3rd are Catholic.

Scouting provides scouts the opportunity to live their own spiritual life within the inter-religious framework that World Scouting offers. Thereby, scouts can help overcome conflicts, build a culture of peace, and build a better world for all.

The First Handbook for Boy Scouts of America printed the first year after its foundation.

There were 300,000 copies of the First Edition, followed three years later with the Second Edition and 3,000,000 copies. Since then there have been nine other editions printed for a total of 36 million copies.

Page 249 of the 1911 Boy Scout Handbook. The very first handbook emphasized the importance of a scouts duty to God, no matter what his religion is.

Chivalry 249

Roman legions laughed in the face of death, and died often with a "Hail, Imperator!" for the Roman Cæsar upon his lips.

One of the stories connected with the battle of Agincourt tells us that four fair ladies had sent their knightly lovers into battle. One of these was killed. Another was made prisoner. The third was lost in the battle and never heard of afterward. The fourth was safe, but owed his safety to shameful flight. "Ah! woe is me," said the lady of this base knight, "for having placed my affections on a coward. He would have been dear to me dead. But alive he is my reproach."

A scout must be as courageous as any knight of old or any Roman soldier or any dying Indian.

Loyalty

Loyalty is another scout virtue which must stand out prominently, because it is that which makes him true to his home, his parents, and his country. Charles VIII, at the Battle of Foronovo, picked out nine of his bravest officers and gave to each of them a complete suit of armor, which was a counterpart of his own. By this device he outwitted a group of his enemies who had leagued themselves to kill him during the fight. They sought him through all the ranks, and every time they met one of these officers they thought they had come face to face with the king. The fact that these officers hailed such a dangerous honor with delight and devotion is a striking illustration of their loyalty.

The scout should be no less loyal to his parents, home, and country.

Duty to God

No scout can ever hope to amount to much until he has learned a reverence for religion. The scout should believe in God and God's word. In the olden days, knighthood, when it was bestowed, was a religious ceremony, and a knight not only considered himself a servant of the king, but also a servant of God. The entire night preceding the day upon which the young esquire was made knight was spent by him on his knees in prayer, in a fast and vigil.

There are many kinds of religion in the world. One important point, however, about them is that they all involve the worship of the same God. There is but one leader, although many ways of following Him. If a scout meets one of another religion, he should remember that he, too, is striving for the best

The First Handbook explains the importance of a scouts' obligation to God. And the first part of the scout oath is to pledge his duty to God. The book encourages the boy scouts individual religious organization to train the Boy Scout in his personal religious life. Below is page 250 in the 1911 Boy Scout Handbook.

250   Boy Scouts

A scout should respect the convictions of others in matters of custom and religion.

A Boy Scout's Religion

The Boy Scouts of America maintain that no boy can grow into the best kind of citizenship without recognizing his obligation to God. The first part of the boy scout's oath or pledge is therefore: "I promise on my honor to do my best to honor my God and my country." The recognition of God as the ruling and leading power in the universe, and the grateful acknowledgement of His favors and blessings is necessary to the best type of citizenship and is a wholesome thing in the education of the growing boy. No matter what the boy may be — Catholic, or Protestant, or Jew — this fundamental need of good citizenship should be kept before him. The Boy Scouts of America therefore recognize the religious element in the training of a boy, but it is absolutely non-sectarian in its attitude toward that religious training. Its policy is that the organization or institution with which the boy scout is connected shall give definite attention to his religious life. If he be a Catholic boy scout, the Catholic Church of which he is a member is the best channel for his training. If he be a Hebrew boy, then the Synagogue will train him in the faith of his fathers. If he be a Protestant, no matter to what denomination of Protestantism he may belong, the church of which he is an adherent or a member should be the proper organization to give him an education in the things that pertain to his allegiance to God. The Boy Scouts of America, then, while recognizing the fact that the boy should be taught the things that pertain to religion, insists upon the boy's religious life being stimulated and fostered by the institution with which he is connected. Of course, it is a fundamental principle of the Boy Scouts of America to insist on

Scout helping old lady across street

The 1911 Boy Scouts of America Handbook pages 14 and 15 show the Scout Oath and the Twelve Points of the Scout Law that are recited at every Scout Meeting right after the Pledge of Allegiance.

14 Boy Scouts

Buttons — The official buttons worn on the scout uniforms sell for 10 cents per set for shirt and 15 cents per set for coat.

Merit Badges — Price 25 cents each.

Boy Scout Certificates — A handsome certificate in two colors, 6 x 8 inches, has been prepared for boy scouts who wish to have a record of their enrolment. The certificate has the Scout Oath and Law and the official Seal upon it, with place for the signature of the scout master. The price is 5 cents.

Directions For Ordering

Important ! When ordering supplies send exact remittance with order. If check is used add New York exchange. Make checks and money orders payable to Boy Scouts of America. All orders received without the proper remittance will be shipped C. O. D., or held until remittance arrives.

The Scout Oath

Before he becomes a scout a boy must promise:

On my honor I will do my best:

1. To do my duty to God and my country, and to obey the scout law;

2. To help other people at all times;

3. To keep myself physically strong, mentally awake, and morally straight.

When taking this oath the scout will stand, holding up his right hand, palm to the front, thumb resting on the nail of the little finger and the other three fingers upright and together.

The Scout Sign

This is the scout sign. The three fingers held up remind him of his three promises in the scout oath.

The Scout Salute

When the three fingers thus held are raised to the forehead, it is the scout salute.

The scout always salutes an officer.

The Scout Law*

There have always been certain written and unwritten laws regulating the conduct and directing the activities of men.

---

*Result of work of Committee on Scout Oath, Scout Law, Tenderfoot, Second-class and First-class Scout Requirements:—
Prof. Jeremiah W. Jenks, Chairman. Dr. Lee K. Frankel, George D. Porter, E. M. Robinson, G. W. Hinckley, B. E. Johnson, Clark W. Hetherington, Arthur A. Carey.

Pages 15 - 16, scout laws

Scoutcraft

We have such unwritten laws coming down from past ages. In Japan, the Japanese have their Bushido or laws of the old Samurai warriors. During the Middle Ages, the chivalry and rules of the Knights of King Arthur, the Knights Templar and the Crusaders were in force. In aboriginal America, the Red Indians had their laws of honor: likewise the Zulus, Hindus, and the later European nations have their ancient codes.

The following laws which relate to the Boy Scouts of America, are the latest and most up to date. These laws a boy promises to obey when he takes his scout oath.

1. A scout is trustworthy.
A scout's honor is to be trusted. If he were to violate his honor by telling a lie, or by cheating, or by not doing exactly a given task, when trusted on his honor, he may be directed to hand over his scout badge.

2. A scout is loyal.
He is loyal to all to whom loyalty is due: his scout leader, his home, and parents and country.

3. A scout is helpful.
He must be prepared at any time to save life, help injured persons, and share the home duties. He must *do at least one good turn to somebody every day.*

4. A scout is friendly.
He is a friend to all and a brother to every other scout.

5. A scout is courteous.
He is polite to all, especially to women, children, old people, and the weak and helpless. *He must not take pay for being helpful or courteous.*

6. A scout is kind.
He is a friend to animals. He will not kill nor hurt any living creature needlessly, but will strive to save and protect all harmless life.

7. A scout is obedient.
He obeys his parents, scout master, patrol leader, and all other duly constituted authorities.

8. A scout is cheerful.
He smiles whenever he can. His obedience to orders is prompt and cheery. He never shirks nor grumbles at hardships.

9. A scout is thrifty.
He does not wantonly destroy property. He works faithfully, wastes nothing, and makes the best use of his oppor-

tunities. He saves his money so that he may pay his own way, be generous to those in need, and helpful to worthy objects.

He may work for pay but must not receive tips for courtesies or good turns.

10. A scout is brave.

He has the courage to face danger in spite of fear and has to stand up for the right against the coaxings of friends or the jeers or threats of enemies, and defeat does not down him.

11. A scout is clean.

He keeps clean in body and thought, stands for clean speech, clean sport, clean habits, and travels with a clean crowd.

12. A scout is reverent.

He is reverent toward God. He is faithful in his religious duties and respects the convictions of others in matters of custom and religion.

The Three Classes of Scouts

There are three classes of scouts among the Boy Scouts of America, the tenderfoot, second-class scout, and first-class scout. Before a boy can become a tenderfoot he must qualify for same. A tenderfoot, therefore, is superior to the ordinary boy because of his training. To be a tenderfoot means to occupy the lowest grade in scouting. A tenderfoot on meeting certain requirements may become a second-class scout, and a second-class scout upon meeting another set of requirements may become a first-class scout. The first-class scout may then qualify for the various merit badges which are offered in another part of this chapter for proficiency in scouting. The requirements of the tenderfoot, second-class scout, and first-class scout, are as follows:

Tenderfoot

To become a scout a boy must be at least twelve years of age and must pass a test in the following:

1. Know the scout law, sign, salute, and significance of the badge.
2. Know the composition and history of the national flag and the customary forms of respect due to it.
3. Tie four out of the following knots: square or reef, sheet-bend, bowline, fisherman's, sheepshank, halter, clove hitch, timber hitch, or two half hitches.

Tenderfoot

A recent article in the 'Scouting' family magazine by Robert Peterson tells about the key role churches and other religious bodies played in scouting's growth. For the first few years, more Scoutmasters were clergymen than any other profession or trade. And still today the religious bodies account for 61 percent of the charter organizations, although the clergymen are no longer the dominate unit leaders. Boy Scouting's promise of outdoor fun and its call on boys to do their duty to God made it an immediate attraction for religious organizations.

James E. West, the first Chief Scout Executive, was responsible for many of the earliest decisions on the establishment of Boy Scouts of America. At his urging the BSA adopted "a Scout is reverent" as the 12th point of the American Scout Law. He explained later, "I felt…that there is nothing more essential in the education of the youth of America than to give them religious instruction." He also stated, "This organization is not Protestant, nor is it Catholic, nor is it Hebrew, but it is a character-building organization for boys, to be used by all religions and institutions, who can see in it a means of helping and assisting the boys of their communities."

Today, the two largest religious bodies involved in Scouting in America are The Church of Jesus Christ of Latter-day Saints (Mormon) and the United Methodist Church. Each has about 400,000 youth members.

Chapter Two

HALE SCOUT RESERVATION

Thanks go to E.H. Shadler, M.D. of McAlester, Oklahoma who recorded the beginnings of Camp Tom Hale. The camp derived its name from Mr. Tom Hale of McAlester, Oklahoma. Mr. Hale started and ran a successful wholesale grocery company in Oklahoma. He became interested in youth work and was the president of the board of the Choctaw Area Council of the Boy Scouts of America for the better part of 22 years from 1919 to 1941. He realized the need for some type of camping facilities and he and his Board of Directors undertook that problem.

A Carlton Weaver of Wilburton, OK was on that board. Carlton Weaver was a newspaper publisher and a state legislator. Carlton owned some land just north of Wilburton known as Robbers Cave. More land was bought and donated by Mr. Hale and others interested in camping and scouting. It was a secluded area and difficult to get to until a Highway was built and finished in 1932. At that time it became an official Boy Scout Camp. Under the guidance of Carlton Weaver the historical land around Camp Tom Hale became a State Park in 1935. It is known as Robbers Cave State Park. In the 1950's the State of Oklahoma offered to trade 480 acres of forest land near Talihina,

Oklahoma for the Boy Scout Camp land & facilities at Robbers Cave.

This land was more suitable for a Boy Scout Camp as it was surrounded by the Quachita National Forest and had a lake perfect for the many waters activities associated with scouting. So the trade was made and in July of 1961, Camp Tom Hale had its first camping season at its present location. Now over 50 different Scouting Merit badges can be earned at Hale Scout Reservation while enjoying the rugged and beautiful scenery of the natural forestland.

CHAPTER THREE

CHAPLAIN LAYMAN DAVID COX OPENING COMMENTS

I was involved in Scouting when I was a boy and became involved again with my son, Andy. Andy and I started attending BSA Camp Tom Hale in 1994. The first few years, the Chapel Services lacked organization. The services were usually handled by one of the college-aged staff members. These young men volunteered their precious time to do this, but often they were just too worn out or had conflicting obligations that kept them from the early morning services. I was very impressed with the Chapel Service when they were held and very disappointed that so few campers were in attendance. Often there were less than a handful of people there.

In 1998, Pastor Jonathan Reichman approached me about becoming involved in rebuilding and reviving the Chapel Service. Jonathan and I were both involved with our sons in Troop 241 in Tulsa. Pastor Reichman, although the Senior Pastor at Riverside Baptist Church, took it upon himself to meet with the area Boy Scout Officials and see if something could be done to restore the attendance of the Chapel Services. So, as it usually happens,

Jonathan was given full responsibility to do just that.

Pastor Reichman realized it was too much for the College students on Staff to have this added responsibility turned over to them and he realized it would be next to impossible to get a member of Clergy to make a commitment of 8 weeks of service at a Summer Scout Camp. His thought and goal was to get 8 people, who were interested enough in the youth of today to make a one-week commitment. I imagine he must have heard me express my feelings about the Chapel Service at Camp Tom Hale, so I was one of the first ones he contacted. When he told me what he had in mind and wanted to know if I would volunteer for one of the weeks at the next summer camp, I was excited, but felt I was not the person. I attend Kirk of the Hills Church in Tulsa, but I explained that I was not a member of the Clergy, I was not an Elder, I was not a Deacon, I was not even on the staff. None of that seemed to faze Jonathan, as he just asked if there was a week that I would be willing to go to HSR. Well, I picked the 2nd week of camp in 1999 and have been going back every summer since then.

I do have a real interest in our youth of today and have attended the Billy Graham school of Evangelism in California, Youth Evangelism Explosion International Training School in Florida and some Youth Discipleship Seminars. I have also been involved with the junior- and senior-high youth at my church for several years. And, I have volunteered at three of the Passion One Day Praise and Worship Gatherings for College Students. Their 3 day gatherings have attracted anywhere from 10,000 to 30,000 college students at one place at one time.

Being a Chaplain at HSR and working with the youth of our country has been a real joy and blessing to me. Those of you already involved with youth in one form or another would say the same thing. For those of you not involved, then I hope this book might be of some encouragement to try it out.

Chapter Four

Introduction to Devotions

You will find my devotions are short and to the point. And there is usually just one main point. One has to realize that these devotions are created to fit the timetable of a uniformly scheduled Boy Scout Camp. Chapel Service is the first item on the daily agenda - even before breakfast. At Hale Scout Reservation the first breakfast was served at 7:30a.m. and so Chapel was set at 7:15a.m. Allowance had to be given for slow arrivals and an ending time that allowed enough time for the scouts to get to the Dining Hall. As a result, that usually left enough time for about a 5-minute devotion.

The Hale Scout Camp Dining Hall was built to seat about 350 campers at a time. It was a new building and it was assumed that this would accommodate all the campers for a meal together at one time for several years. In just a couple of years, however, camp attendance was reaching over 350 campers a week, so a split dining hall schedule was instituted. The first group was served at 7:30 and the second group to be served about 30 minutes later. At that time the Scout Masters suggested a double chapel service also, so the second Chapel started at 7:45a.m. In 2006, camp attendance was over 800 campers a week.

The following devotions are just a guide. The way I set up my Chapel Service was left up to me. Other Chaplains could set up their Chapel Service any way they wanted to, but we were all aware of the time limitations. And whenever we let Chapel run too long, we were sure to hear about it from the Scout Masters or the Camp Director. I always start by playing some contemporary music first and continue it until I feel most of the Scout Troops have arrived. During this time I'm also looking for some Scouts who would like to volunteer to help me. I need some scouts to pass out Song Sheets that have the words printed on them for the music that is being played that morning. I'm also looking for a scout or two who would read the scripture or scriptures for the day. Sometimes I need some scouts to help during the devotion with props that are to be used. And then, after the closing, I need some scouts to help pass out trinkets or novelties that are analogous or representative of the days devotional message. Occasionally, I'll have a scout come up to me and ask if he can do the closing prayer. What a thrill that is, and of course any scout that will ask me that, I'll grant his request without any qualm whatsoever. It is my intent to get as many scouts as possible involved in Chapel Services one way or another.

The particular songs and music that I play, I pick because they too may tie into the message for the day. And that is another reason why I like the printed song sheets, so that the scouts can see the words and see how they co-mingle with the devotion message. By the way, I avoid using the words, "sermon", "preaching", and "worship", knowing full well that these words are not the best words to use if I'm trying to encourage scouts to come to Chapel. I feel words like "devotion", "praise", "service", and "message" are more inviting. So, the first day when I'm talking to the scout masters, I encourage them to bring their scouts to the short morning chapel service or message, etc. The knick-knacks or give-aways should relate to the message of the day also. They do not need to be expensive or elaborate, and it has surprised me what an important part they play. Scouts and the adult leaders often save each one and attach them to their hats or clothing. Other scouts, who were not at chapel, then ask them what that item is. And most of the scouts will be able to tell them about the message of the day. Some troops have a chapel service of their own later that night and ask the scout chaplain's aide to present the message of the day to the scouts who were unable to attend the morning service. It pleases me when I can get up to 50% of the campers to attend a chapel service and then have the others come up to me later and ask for one of the give-away items and explain that they were not at chapel but heard about the message. For this reason I have to be sure and wear cargo shorts so that I can have some extra give-away items in my pockets.

The Devotions or messages I'm mentioning here are some of the ones I've used over the last 7 years. Some of them will be dated by something that had just recently happened to me or to our country. So, they would not be timely to be used again. But I've listed them so that you can see how you can use current events to come up with your own devotions.

Chapter Five

Favorite Devotions

Title: KEEPING AWAY THE ELEPHANTS

Opening Prayer

Scripture: New Testament, Philippians 4: 4-8 (This is when Paul is talking about joy even while he is in prison.)

> *4/ Always be full of joy in the Lord. I say it again- rejoice! 5/ Let everyone see that you are considerate in all you do. Remember, the Lord is coming soon. 6/ Don't worry about anything; instead, pray about everything. Tell God what you need and thank Him for all He has done. 7/ If you do this, you will experience God's peace. Which is far more wonderful than the human mind can understand......8/ And now.....let me say one more thing as I close this letter. Fix your thoughts on what is true and honorable and right. Think about things that are pure and lovely and admirable. Think about things that are excellent and worthy of praise.*

Chapter Five

Old Testament, Psalm 3:5

> *I lay down and slept. I woke up in safety, for the Lord was watching over me.*

Message: I was just in Hugo, Oklahoma, which has been the winter Headquarters for some Circus Companies over the years. They even have a cemetery there where circus performers are buried and have some unusual headstones shaped like circus animals or circus tents. I got to talk to someone from Hugo who told me about two 1000 pound elephants that escaped a few years back and they couldn't be found for almost 3 months.

It reminded me of a story about the guy sitting on a bench in a park like one in your home town. He was tearing up paper into little pieces and throwing them on the ground. A stranger came up and asked him what he was doing and he said he was keeping the elephants away. The stranger said…Well, there aren't any elephants around here. "Exactly," said the guy, "it works."

Imagine never worrying about anything. It's probably a impossibility - we all have worries on the job, in our home, at school, maybe here at Scout camp. But here Paul is saying to turn our worries into prayers. Whenever you start to worry, stop and pray.

God's peace is different. Sometimes we can find peace through positive thinking or from distancing ourselves from a problem, BUT TRUE Peace comes from prayer and knowing that God is in control.

What you put into your mind determines what or how you think. Be careful of what you put into your mind - through TV, books, music, movies, magazines, and computers. Be sure God would approve - and if you're not sure - Ask Him in your prayers.

And don't spend a lot of energy worrying about the "What-Ifs". What if an elephant came charging in here? Take your "what-ifs" to God- He is in control.

Sometimes you might feel like you're spinning around in a circle and just don't know what to do or where to go. Go to God. And to help you remember this I've got something for you that might help, which I will give you right after our closing prayer.

Closing Prayer

Reminder Item: unshelled peanuts

Associated Music: Darrel Evans, "Trading My Sorrows"

Title: CRACKED POT

Opening Prayer

Scripture: New Testament, Ephesians 4:2 [This was a letter written by Paul while he was in prison in Rome. The purpose of the letter was to encourage and strengthen the people in Ephesus who were believers in Jesus Christ.]

> *4:2 Be Humble and gentle. Be patient with each other, making allowance for each other's faults.....*

Old Testament, Ezra 5:2 [This book written by Ezra around 450BC and the purpose was to show God's faithfulness and how His prophets were sent to encourage and strengthen his people.]

> *5:2 Zerubbabel and Jeshua begin the task of rebuilding the Temple of God in Jerusalem. And the prophets of God were with them and helped them.*

Message: There is a story about a cracked pot, it is an East Indian Fable. A servant was responsible for bringing fresh water to the master's house each day. He would walk two miles every morning to a well and fill two pots that he carried on a long pole on his back, a pot on each end of the long pole. One pot was cracked and would only be half full by the time the servant returned to the master's house. It bothered the pot. So one day the pot asked the servant to replace him because he was not any good…only got back with half a pot of water.

    The servant told the pot not to worry and just enjoy the walk back to the master's house and look at the flowers along the way. When they arrived at the master's house the pot was still distressed, and asked the servant to replace him. The servant said, well didn't you see the beautiful flowers. The pot said yes but it didn't make him feel any better. The servant then said "Well you don't understand. You noticed the flowers were all on your side of the path. I was aware of your fault so I planted flower seeds along your side of the path and everyday you watered them. I now pick some flowers every day and put them on the master's table and the master loves the flowers.

I'd like to tell you about a scout who was in my troop (Troop 241 in Tulsa). His name is Todd Houston, and around 20 years ago he lost a leg at age 14 in a freak water skiing accident. He stayed calm and did not panic, even though the doctors said he died three times from loss of blood. With just one leg, you might think he'd feel like he couldn't do a lot of things anymore. But Todd continued on in scouting and became an Eagle Scout. Not only did he become an Eagle Scout but he continued on with a passion for mountain climbing. As a matter of fact he set a United States record of climbing the highest peak or elevation in all of the 50 states in the shortest time ever. He climbed the highest spot in every one of the 50 states in only 64 days. And the almost unbelievable part of this achievement is that he beat the previous record by 46 days. The previous record of 110 days was held by a healthy two-legged man.

This week at camp, we want to help you find something that you excel at. Some of you will discover, for the first time, something that you're very good at and you never knew it.

CLOSING PRAYER

Reminder Item: Paper Cup representing water pot

Associated Music: Big Tent Revival and "What Would Jesus Do"

Title: Ants, Coneys, Locusts, Lizards, and Frogs

Question to Scouts: Is there anyone here this morning who is taking the Insect or Reptile or Mammal Merit Badge Class? Well, today we're going to talk about ants, locusts, lizards, frogs, and coneys. All are mentioned in the Bible.

Opening Prayer

Scripture and Message: Most of today's message ties in to the Book of Proverbs. The purpose of Proverbs is to teach us how to attain wisdom and how to do what is right and just.

Old Testament: Proverbs 30:24-25

> *24/ There are four things on earth that are small but unusually wise: 25/ Ants- they aren't strong, but they store up food for the winter.*

Also, Ants are mentioned in Proverbs 6: 6-8

> *6/ Take a lesson from the ants. Learn from their ways and be wise! 7/ Even though they have no one ruling over them to make them work, 8/ they labor hard all summer, gathering food for the winter.*

So the ants can teach us about being prepared. So here at camp this week, work hard and study hard, because what you learn now will help determine what you will have in the future.

Proverbs 30:26 refers to coneys (also known as Rock badgers). They look like an overgrown guinea pig.

> *26/ they are powerful, but they make their homes among the rocky cliffs.*

So likewise, we should learn from the coneys to build our life on a good foundation of God and faith and then we too will have a safe place.

> *Proverbs 30:27 The Locusts do not have a king, and yet they march like an army in ranks.*

The locusts advance because they make good friends and they work together. So we too, need to be wise in who we make friends with and who we hang with. Make some good friends while you're here at camp. Believers in Christ will be supporters for life.

Proverbs 30:28 talks about lizards.

> *28/ Lizards are easy to catch, but they are found even in a king's palace.*

So as the lizard is content to live life where ever it may be- we too should be content where we are and not worry or fret. Turn your worries over to God.
    And finally, Frogs. Usually when frogs are mentioned in the Bible, it has something to do with a plague. But we can use the letters of FROG to remind us to Fully Rely On God.

CLOSING PRAYER

Reminder Item: Plastic Lizards

Associated Music: DC Talk 'Jesus Freak'

Title: HORSES AND MULES

Opening Prayer

Scripture: Old Testament, Psalm 32: 8-9 The Psalms are a type of poetry that generally express praise and worship to God. David wrote this particular Psalm.

8/ The Lord says, "I will guide you along the best pathway for your life. I will advise you and watch over you. 9/ Do not be like a senseless horse or mule that needs a bit and bridle to keep it under control."

I was talking to Dennis Austin here Sunday night. Dennis heads up the Horsemanship Merit Badge Class and the trail rides. He was saying there are 2 ways to break-in a new horse. 1) using discipline and punishment with bits and bridles (the way he used to do it until about 10 years ago) or 2) the way he does it now after reading a book by Monti Roberts called "Whispering to Horses" where you use love and wisdom.

Dennis says that horses that are trained with love and wisdom are much better than horses trained with punishment. Some of us are like horses and mules (we're stubborn). And rather than letting God guide us with His love and wisdom - God has to use discipline and punishment. So that we can be a better person, lets have God train us and guide us with His Love & Wisdom.

From the song we heard a while ago, "Saddle Up Your Horses", Steven Curtis Chapman, who is from Kentucky, is telling us that maybe we've done some things in the past that we weren't happy about. Maybe we've been stubborn and have upset someone and we carry this burden of guilt. But he reminds us that God forgives us and He loves us. And when we understand that, then our lives are changed and we'll never be the same. Every day will be great. No more life with a long-face. So, come on – Today. Believe in Gods Grace, Saddle up and get ready for the ride of your life.

CLOSING PRAYER

Reminder Item: 2 ½" small asst'd horses

Associated Music: The Great Adventure CD by Steven Curtis Chapman and the song "Saddle up Your Horses".

Title: FOX AT THE CROSS

Opening Prayer

Scripture Reading: Old Testament, Judges 15:4

> *Then he (Samson) went out and caught three hundred foxes. He tied their tails together in pairs, and he fastened a lit torch to each pair of tails.*

Song of Songs 2:15

> *"Quick! Catch all the little foxes before they ruin the vineyard..."*

New Testament, Luke 13:32 Jesus is talking here about Herod.

> *32/ "Go tell that fox that I will keep on casting out demons and doing miracles of healing."*

I go to a church in Tulsa that is pretty well centrally located. The area it is in has been fully developed for years with houses and office buildings all around it, and busy thoroughfares on two sides of it. The church is expanding right now and there is a lot of construction going on. Because of our cramped and confined area we are even building a two-level parking area.

In the midst of all this hustle and bustle though, the church has left a little patch of hillside (no larger that your average house lot) in a natural state. A couple of Eagle Scout projects have enhanced the area. One Eagle Scout cleared a trail up to the cross and then another Scout built 4 wood benches there.

A couple of weeks ago, I and three other church members decided to meet at that cross early one morning, to have a devotional, some prayer and to pray for our church. As one member was starting to pray we saw a small, wild, red fox casually walk by us (not more than 20 feet away). The fox didn't bother to look at us but just walked by and on down the hill away from the cross and out of our sight. Why the fox was there we have no idea! Did God plan it?? Maybe so! The fox looked like what they call a cross phase red fox which is reddish brown in color with a black band across the shoulders and a black line down the back, which forms a cross. Hummm- a cross on a fox at the Cross. Makes you kinda wonder!

From the scripture we heard earlier we see that the Bible mentions foxes several times - usually in the context of being devious, cunning and misleading. In the New Testament in Luke, Jesus compared Herod (A Roman Ruler) to a fox, because of his crafty, devious nature. In the Old Testament in the Book of Judges it talks about Samson using 300 foxes to help destroy the Philistines fields. Samson tied the foxes tails together in pairs and then set a torch to their tails and sent them running through the fields setting them on fire and destroying all the grain and vineyards of the Philistines.

Again in the Old Testament- in the book Song of Songs, the young women of Jerusalem are warned: "Quick! Catch all the little foxes before they ruin the vineyard..." What the author here was implying, was that little problems in our lives can ruin relationships - little problems in a church can destroy it too. So today I'm telling you, we want you to have a great time here at summer camp and if you have some little problems bothering you, some little foxes getting in your way, then PRAY and chase them away. Don't let the little things ruin your good times here at camp.

Closing Prayer

Reminder Item: Glow Cross, Neon Cross Necklace or Cross Key Chain

Chapter Five

NOTE- The previous day to this message I passed out some rolls of fake money to about 10 scouts. I asked them to pass out the money during the day to other scouts, merit badge instructors, cafeteria help, adult leaders, and anyone who they felt had done something special in the way of helping them or others. In other words, I wanted them to encourage and reward anyone who best exemplified the Scout Law.

TITLE: WHO WANTS TO BE A MILLIONAIRE

OPENING PRAYER

Scripture Reading: Old Testament Psalm 37:21

> *The wicked borrow and never repay, but the Godly are generous givers.*

Today we're going to talk about MONEY. The Bible talks about money several times. The first time it is mentioned is in the Old Testament in the first book of the Bible in Genesis. Gen 17:13. This is where God is telling Abraham that every male shall be circumcised and God says:

> *"every male born in your house and every male servant bought with your money."*

How many of you have watched the TV show "Who Wants to be a Millionaire?" You know the basics then…Regis Philbin starts off with some easy questions and the questions get harder as the amount of money you can win gets bigger. You have "3 Life Lines" that you can use in the course of questions… And they are?
 1) 50/50 (Where two possible answers are eliminated)
 2) The Audience Poll
 3) Someone of your choice you can call on the phone for help.

We can apply this TV show to our daily lives….
 As we go through life we will find there are good and easy times and then there are bad and tough times. Some of those times we will know what

to do and just do it without any help. Other times we may have to decide between several choices - eliminating some and then guessing on the rest (50/50). Sometimes when things get tough we'll have to ask others for help (our schoolmates, co-workers, friends, etc.). We'll take a poll. And then we'll have to hope they guided us the right way. Usually they do, but every now and then even they will be wrong. And then when the questions or life's problems get really tough- Like on the Millionaire....we need to call on our ULTIMATE Lifeline- God. We need to call on Him in Prayer. Our Heavenly God is never wrong and always knows the answer, whereas our earthly friends are sometimes wrong or do not know the answer.

There's another place in the Bible (Luke 19) that is a parable or story about the king who gave ten pounds of silver to ten of his servants and asked them to increase the size of his kingdom while he was gone. Some had 10-fold the increase, some 5-fold, and some had no increase.

Those ten scouts who we gave money to yesterday- I have a couple of questions...

How many of you gave away all of your money ($10,000)? Some of you still have some then?

I hope no one still has all $10,000, because that means either you didn't find anyone worthy or you didn't do your part in helping to encourage others.

Today, everyone here is going to get some of this $4 million I have to give away. I want each one of you to then pass it on to others - to encourage and reward those who best exemplify the Scout Law. And all of you should be getting money back too, by helping others and doing something special. What we want to do is increase the number of people here at Tom Hale who are living up to the Scout Law by being helpful, courteous, kind, cheerful, and friendly. This will please you and God.

CLOSING PRAYER

Reminder Item: Stage Money

Associated Music: 'Awesome God' by Rich Mullins, 'Cartoon Song' by Chris Rice

Title: THE EAGLES ARE LANDING

Opening Prayer

Scripture Reading: Old Testament Deuteronomy 32:11

> 'Like an eagle that rouses' her chicks and hovers over her young, so he spread his wings to take them in and carried them aloft on his pinons.

Old Testament, Isaiah 40:31

> But those who wait (or hope) on the Lord will find new strength. They will fly high on wings like eagles....'

Question: Anyone here taking the Astronomy Merit Badge? Who here is interested in traveling in outer space or in space exploration? Well, let me give you a hint on what could help you achieve that goal.

Answer: Of the 12 Astronauts to walk on the moon, 11 had something in common. They had all been involved in Scouting.

Last December, our Troop visited the Space Museum in Hutchinson, Kansas. If your troop hasn't done that yet - I highly recommend it. If scouts have the time & interest they can also earn some merit badges there - including the Space Exploration Merit Badge.

Here at Tom Hale our goal is to help each one of you to become an Eagle Scout. Some of you may even be participating in the 'Soaring to Eagle' program here. The Eagle in scouting symbolizes power, strength, swiftness & endurance.

In the Bible, God uses the Eagle to symbolize the same thing. The Golden Eagle has a wing span of 8 feet and the mother eagle will carry her young on her back until the eaglet masters the art of flying. In the Book of Deuteronomy, Moses used this familiar picture from nature to describe God's care for His people. Moses describes God here:

> *"Like an eagle that rouses her chicks and hovers over them. God so spread His wings to take them in and carried them aloft on His pinons (or wings)."* God carried the people of Israel safely on His wings to take them from slavery in Egypt.

In Isaiah, we hear:

> *"Those who wait on the Lord will find new strength. They will fly high on wings like eagles."* Here the author Prophet Isaiah, is telling the people in Judah that there will be times when they will grow tired of their problems & troubles. They will be weak and worn out, but if they turn to God and trust in Him, He will renew their strength to where they will be able to run and even feel like they are flying like an eagle.

There may be times here at camp or times after you get home that you just feel worn out. Times when you feel loaded down with problems. When you get to feeling that way, turn to God in prayer - tell Him you're tired and worn out and ask Him to lift you up and renew your hope and strength.

Today- to remind you of God's wings and to remind you of the people here at Camp Tom Hale who want to help you become an Eagle, we've got an eagle for each one of you to have which we'll pass out right after this closing prayer.

CLOSING PRAYER

Reminder Item: Small plastic eagle

Associated Music: 'Freedom' on Freedom CD by Darrell Evans

NOTE- Before September 11, 2001, I used this Devotional Message to get across the importance of calling on God when we need help. After 9/11, I no longer used this devotional. I cannot explain why I haven't used it or why I haven't revised it and updated it to include what happened on 9/11/2001. It may be that the timing of that event and the tragedy of it made too much of a spiritual and emotional impact on me. Even now, as I write this, it is very difficult to express my feelings. Perhaps you or someone else reading this book will be able to use this devotional and include the events of 9/11/2001.

TITLE: 911

OPENING PRAYER

Question: Has anyone here ever had to call 911?

We've learned about calling 911 in some of our Merit Badge classes such as: Emergency Preparation, First Aid, and CPR. We know that dialing 911 will get us emergency help anywhere in the U.S.…and now in many countries of the world.

Story…In a case I read about recently, a young man and his car had been hijacked (he was probably a Boy Scout because he didn't panic). He dialed 911 on his cell phone without the hijacker knowing, and he let the police dispatcher listen in while he gave clues about his location. And the police were able to apprehend the hijacker.

In emergencies, like this example, all we have to do is punch in three numbers on a phone. Many times though the help we need we can't get from picking up a phone and dialing 911.

The help we need comes from a different 911. We can find that help in Scripture….Psalm 91. 91:1 and 91:15. In this Psalm, the point is that God doesn't promise a world free of danger, but he does promise his help whenever we face danger.

> 91:1 says, "Those who live in the shelter of the Most High will find rest in the shadow of the Almighty."

91:15 is where God says,

> "When they call on me, I will answer. I will be with them in trouble..."

Who selected 911 as the numbers to call for help? Why were the numbers 9-1-1 picked? What do you think? Do you think when the phone company was looking for a special number for people to use when help was needed - maybe, just maybe, they got a little help in what number to use. Or could it have been just a coincidence.

The next time you need some special help- Dial Psalm 91:1.
And whenever you hear #911- let it be a reminder of Psalm 91:1

Closing Prayer

Reminder Item: The Phos Cross and a short explanation: this cross gets its strength from light. The closer and longer it is next to light- the brighter and longer it will glow. That is like our lives. We get our source of strength from God. The closer and longer we get next to God, the brighter we will glow.

Associated Music:

Title: MUSIC, MUSIC, MUSIC

Opening Prayer

Scripture Reading: Old Testament, Psalm 81:2-3

> 2/ Sing! Beat the tambourine, Play the sweet lyre and the harp. 3/ Sound the trumpet for a second feast...

Old Testament, Psalm 150: 3-6 (This is the Last Psalm and it is a closing song of praise) it says:

> 3/ Praise him with a blast of the trumpet; praise him with the lyre and harp! 4/ Praise him with the tambourine and dancing: praise him with stringed instruments and flutes! 5/ Praise him with a clash of cymbals; praise him with loud clanging cymbals. 6/ Let everything that lives sing praise to the Lord!

In different Church Denominations, and even in different churches within the same Denomination, people may Praise or Hymn to God in different ways. Myself and most of the youth in our church like music that is upbeat and lively that is found in our Contemporary Service. I like this music just before the Preacher starts or before we pray. Music you like prepares you, gets you in the right frame of mind, gets you ready to enjoy the message and to help you understand it.

The Bible mentions all kinds of musical instruments like: harps, lyres, cymbals, bells, trumpets, horns, and tambourines.

In the book of 1 Samuel, chapter 16, it tells about King Saul and how he would have terrible depressions and fears and that only the music of a harp could soothe his mind.

Does the music you play or listen to have a negative or positive impact upon your relationship with God?

Sometimes it's not just the sound of the music but it's the words you are listening to that can have a negative or detrimental influence on you. A couple of the worst Country Music Song Titles I've heard are: "If Love Was Oil I'd be a Quart Low" or "I'm Just a Bug on the Windshield of Life" hmmm…. not too thrilling thinking of yourself as a squashed juicy bug on somebody's windshield is it?

I like to make a comparison of music to the lessons you get before you dive into the water. You can read about diving, watch some films, get some instruction, do some stretching exercises, climb up the ladder to the diving board, walk out to the edge of the board, do a couple of bounces… and then you dive in. Good music gets you prepared and primed for a Godly message.

Well, the Staff here at Tom Hale and the merit badge instructors are like the music- Before they let you shoot any arrows, or shoot the rifles, or ski down the slope - they are going to prepare you- they will teach you, let you touch the equipment, let you get the feel- So, when the time is right, you'll feel Great and do Great at the targets, or the slope, or whatever you get to do.

To help remind you of today's message, we've got a kazoo for each one of you to have and we'll pass them out right after this closing prayer.

CLOSING PRAYER

Reminder Item: Kazoo

Associated Music: From Passion, 'You have done Great Things' and 'Dance in the River'

Title: BAD BUFO

Opening Prayer

Scripture Reading: Old Testament, 1 Samuel 13:11-12

> *11/ but Samuel said, "What is this you have done?" Saul replied, "I saw my men scattering from me, and you didn't arrive when you said you would, and the Philistines are at Micmash ready for battle. 12/ So I said, 'The Philistines are ready to march against us, and I haven't even asked for the Lord's help!' So I felt obliged to offer the burnt offering myself before you came."*

The theme of this story in the scripture today is about Samuel and Saul (Samuel was the Last Judge, or Prophet, under God's Authority) and Saul (was the First King of Israel). Well Saul had a big problem and he got impatient with God's timing and so he took things into his own hands. As a result, Saul's problems got worse.

In the early 1900's, some biologist in South Florida had a problem with some pests that were ruining the sugar cane fields. The biologist quickly came up with the idea to import some huge South American toads (called Bufo Marinus and also known as 'Giant Toads'). They were twice as large as most toads….weighing over three pounds. It seemed like a good idea, but it didn't work out.

To no ones surprise, these toads reproduced like all toads do, laying eggs in the thousands. But what was not known at the time is that these toads are dog-killers. If a dog or another animal ate one of these toads, it got a mouthful of poisonous white gunk that was poisonous enough to kill many of them. Often, our efforts to "fix" a problem in our lives may backfire just as badly as bringing these toads into Florida did.

When faced with a problem, don't allow impatience to take control. Pray to God and ask for His help. God often uses delays to test our obedience and patience. How do you handle those tough situations where you feel you are in a panic? Here at Camp maybe you're feeling like you're not going to pass or get that Merit Badge, so you feel like you'll have to copy, or cheat, or just quit. The best solution is to do what is right and trust God. Then ask for help from your instructor, Scoutmaster, or assistant Scoutmaster. It's the right way to do it and in the long run, it's the only way to do it.

To help remind you of today's lesson we've got a Bufo to give to you right after this closing prayer.

Closing Prayer

Reminder Item: Colorful Rainforest Frogs

Associated Music:

Title: "Let's Roll"

Opening Prayer

Scripture Reading: Old Testament, Psalm 93: 1-5

> 1/ The Lord is king! He is robed in majesty. Indeed, the Lord is robed in majesty and armed with strength. The world is firmly established; it cannot be shaken. 2/ Your throne, O Lord, has been established from time immemorial. You yourself are from the everlasting past. 3/ The mighty oceans have roared, O Lord. The mighty oceans roar like thunder; the mighty oceans roar as they pound the shore. 4/ But mightier than the violent raging of seas, mightier than the breakers on the shore- the Lord above is mightier than these! 5/ Your royal decrees cannot be changed. The nature of your reign, O Lord, is holiness forever.

Does the name Todd Beamer mean anything to you? Does Psalm 93 or United Airlines Flight 93 help?

Until Sept.11th, 2001, very few people had heard of Todd Beamer. Now, if you type in his name on the web it brings up almost 15,000 results. Todd became a national hero because of what had before Sept.11th been an unimaginable incident. Because of his 13 minute conversation with a GTE telephone operator, Lisa Thompson, we can get a glimpse of his situation and how he handled it. There were several other heroes on that same plane and several of them were also talking on their cell phones. Todd was the only one though who was talking to a total stranger. The others had called friends and loved ones. Todd could have called his wife too (another Lisa by the way) but it is figured he felt he thought it was better to talk to someone who would be less emotional and someone who would have had some training in this situation.

In his conversation Todd was able to assess the situation and was able to figure out these hi-jackers were not just stealing the plane to ask for ransom, but were going to fly the plane probably into the White House or some other prominent structure like the Statue of Liberty or the Congressional Building. He realized he was going to die but he knew he had to do something to keep others from being killed. Todd was a strong believer and he trusted God. He asked the operator to repeat the Lord's Prayer with him and then he started quoting the 23rd Psalm:

> 1/ The Lord is my shepherd; I have everything I need. 2/ He lets me rest in green meadows; he leads me beside peaceful streams. 3/ He renews my strength. He guides me along right paths, bringing honor to his name. 4/ Even when I walk through the dark valley of death, I will not be afraid, for you are close beside me. Your rod and your staff protect and comfort me. 5/ You prepare a feast for me in the presence of my enemies. You welcome me as a guest anointing my head with oil. My cup overflows with blessings. 6/ Surely, your goodness and unfailing love will pursue me all the days of my life, and I will live in the house of the Lord forever.

Todd was a man of action, he was brought up being taught to be a leader, to trust in God and to take action when action was needed. We can learn a lot from Todd. We can learn that when we are faced with a situation that is frightening beyond our imagination, that if we know God and feel that God is prompting us to get up and get involved, that God will be with us when we take action. Todd's last five words included the last two that have become familiar around the world… "Let's Roll". These two words have been the rallying cry of many of our Brave men and women in Afghanistan and around the world. Todd's father has pointed out though, the importance of the three words just before "Let's Roll", and those words were, "Are You Ready".

Here at Camp Hale, the Staff, the Leaders, your Scout Masters and myself all are helping you to learn to be Leaders. Do not take lightly anything you are being taught here, but learn everything to the best of your ability. We want you to be ready when God needs you. And if you feel you're not spiritually ready for when God calls you, then talk to me sometime while you're at camp this week. Now let's get ready to "Roll".

Closing Prayer

Reminder Item: Tootsie Roll

Title: Tough Trees

Opening Prayer

Scripture Reading: New Testament Romans 5:3-4 (This is Paul's letter to the Christians in Rome. He says…)

> *3/ We can rejoice too, when we run into problems and trials, for we know that they are good for us - they help us learn to endure. 4/ And endurance develops strength of character in us, and character strengthens our confident expectation of salvation.*

New Testament James 1: 2-4

> *2/ When trouble comes your way, let it be an opportunity for learning and joy 3/ For when your faith is tested, your endurance has a chance to grow. 4/ So let it grow, for when your endurance is fully developed, you will be strong in character and ready for anything.*

Comment to Scripture Readings: We do not need to pretend to be happy when we face pain and problems - But we should have a positive outlook. The trouble can help us learn to endure with God's Help. It will make our character stronger and help us to be ready for anything.

I don't know if you've heard of the Bristlecone Pine trees or not because they're found growing mainly on top of the mountains in the Western part of the United States and at elevations of 10,000 to 11,000 feet. They are the world's oldest living trees. Many are estimated to be three- to four-thousand years old. They survive extremely harsh conditions such as artic temperatures, fierce winds, thin air, and little rainfall. But this hardship has produced extraordinary strength and staying power.

Well, right here in this part of Oklahoma and only 4 or 5 miles from right here are some trees with a similar background. They live on the higher elevations of these Kiamichi Mountains of which this camp site is in. They are called Drawf Trees and you can see them as you drive along Highway 1 or Talimena Drive. When you first see them you think they are young trees that have just been planted- But in reality, these trees are subjected to many of the same harsh conditions as the Bristlecone Pines- only on a smaller scale. These trees are actually 100's of years old but are only 5 or 6 feet tall. They are subjected to cold weather, sleet and hail, fierce winds, and a lack of water. The tops of these mountains consist mainly of highly porous rocks and when it rains the moisture drains down through the rocks very quickly, leaving very little moisture for the trees. These 5- and 6- foot trees have developed roots though, that are 20, 30, and 40 feet deep…seeking the moisture.

So as James tells us, we too should expect trouble and harsh conditions in our lives and maybe even here this week at camp, BUT with God with us we will endure and have the joy of knowing we will be even stronger in the days and years ahead of us.

Today, I brought a few pine cones for each of the troops to help remind them of today's story and for everybody else there is a snicker bar with nuts in it, and since nuts come from trees…maybe it will remind you of the tough trees.

Closing Prayer

Reminder Item: Some pine cones and miniature Snicker bars

Associated Music:

Title: 'War'

Opening Prayer

Scripture Reading: Old Testament, Joshua 23: 9-11 Joshua was a brilliant military leader and the key to his success was his submission to God. When God spoke, Joshua listened and obeyed. Here Joshua is telling the leaders of Israel-

> 9/ *"For the Lord has driven out great and powerful nations for you, and no one has yet been able to defeat you. 10/ Each one of you will put to flight a thousand of the enemy, for the Lord your God fights for you, just as he has promised. 11/ So be very careful to love the Lord your God."*

New Testament, 1 Timothy 1:18 The author of Timothy was Paul. Paul wrote this letter to give encouragement to Timothy and all believers everywhere. Paul writes,

> *18/ Timothy, here are my instructions for you, … May they give you the confidence to fight well in the Lord's battles.*

How many of you are familiar with the card game 'War'? Maybe some of you are playing it here at camp even. If you're not familiar with it, then let me tell you. The object of the game is to win everyone else's cards. If 2, 3 or more are playing, all the cards are dealt out evenly to each person face down. Then each player turns a card over and the highest card takes all those cards. I was watching some boys playing at Sunday school awhile back and one boy kept winning. I asked the other boys why this one kid kept winning and they said he was always being dealt most of the Ace's (the highest card). Those of you, who have played before, tell me…What are the chances of winning the game if you're dealt ALL 4 Aces?? Pretty good aren't they? To be dealt all 4 aces would make you feel confident wouldn't it? Oh sure, you might lose a few cards here and there, but in the long run, you know you're going to win.

Well, when you have God (Jesus) in your life, it's like having all four aces. You're going to end up winning. Again, along the way you may have some let downs, some loses, but you'll have the confidence, and knowledge, and peace of knowing that you're going to be the eventual winner.

So, Joshua, the great military leader and faithful servant of God, was in the position to tell the Israelites that WITH GOD, no one will be able to defeat you. For the Lord your God fights for you. So be loyal in your love to God. If you're not for sure you have got the four aces (or God) in your life and you want to, then get with me sometime while you are here at camp and I'll give you that assurance.

To help remind you of today's story, I've got some playing cards (or soldiers) to give you right after our closing prayer.

Closing Prayer

Reminder Items: Miniature Deck of Cards or Toy Soldiers

Associated Music: "The Only Thing I Need" by 4HIM

Title: THE SIMPLIFIED BIBLE

Opening Prayer

Scripture Reading: New Testament, Matthew 28:19 Matthew wrote this book to the Jews and he wanted to prove that Jesus is the Messiah. Here in this scripture Matthew quotes the last words Jesus told him and the other disciples. Jesus says,

> 19/ "Therefore, go and make disciples of all nations, baptizing them in the name of the Father, and the Son and the Holy Spirit.
> This is called Jesus Great Commission (or assignment) to us.

Questions: What does UPS stand for? (United Parcel Services)
What about BSA? (Boy Scouts of America)
What about SARS? (Severe Acute Respiratory Syndrome)
What about WWJD? (What Would Jesus Do)
What about BIBLE? (Basic Instructions Before Leaving Earth)

When I was growing up my mother made sure I went to church every Sunday. I never was too thrilled about it, and I never really understood what the Pastor was talking about, and I couldn't figure out what the Bible was all about. I had other things on my mind. After college though, I decided I'd read the Bible from front to back so I could figure out what it was all about. Here you've got a book that is about 2000 pages long, the words are in small print, and there are no pictures. After spending a couple of years reading it (and reading it in the King James Version at that), I was more confused than ever. Well some years later I tried again and I had the same result again.

Finally, one day I was talking to someone about it and he said: "Hey, there's one sentence in there that tells you what the main theme is, or what the main purpose is, or why it was written. It's right there in First John 5:13,

> 'These things (or these words or this book) I have written to you...
> so that you may know you have eternal life.' Period. That's it." This Book, all these words are written so that you may know you have eternal life!

After thousands and thousands of words and over 2000 pages, two sentences simplify the whole Bible.

But Now….we have to do some more. Just like this Fishing Merit Badge Book, where it says right here in the very front:

The secret to successfully earning the Fishing Merit Badge is for you to use both the pamphlet and the suggestions of your counselor. Your counselor can be as important to you as a coach is to an athlete. Use all of the resources your counselor can make available to you. Your instructor (an experienced fisherman) here at camp can quickly tell you that this book is about fishing. And he can quickly tell you that to catch a fish you will need a rod and reel and bait. But there is a whole lot more he's going to tell you and show you to help you catch a fish.

It's the same thing about your faith and the Bible. You need to read it, study it, listen to your pastor, youth ministers and other experienced Christians. And now, if there is anyone here who wants to be sure they are going to have eternal life, get with me while we're here at camp.

Today, to help you remember what we've talked about, I've got a fish for each of you.

Closing Prayer

Reminder Item: a plastic fish

Associated Music: "BIBLE" by Burlap to Cashmere
"WWJD" by Big Tent Revival

Chapter Five

TITLE: **THE SHEPHERD AND THE SNAKES**

OPENING PRAYER

Scripture Reading: Old Testament, Psalm 23: 1-5

> 1/ The Lord is my shepherd; I have everything I need. 2/ He lets me rest in green meadows; he leads me beside peaceful streams. 3/ He renews my strength. He guides me along right paths, bringing honor to his name. 4/ Even when I walk through the dark valley of death, I will not be afraid, for you are close beside me. Your rod and your staff protect and comfort me. 5/ You prepare a feast for me in the presence of my enemies. You welcome me as a guest, anointing my head with oil.

I read a book recently by Haddon Robinson (Haddon is regarded as one of the greatest Preachers of the twentieth century). The book was called, 'Trusting the Shepherd'. Haddon explains that David (who wrote the 23rd Psalm) was a shepherd and in this psalm David is referring to God as his Shepherd and he and we are the sheep. As some of you may have heard before, sheep aren't very bright, as a matter of fact they're pretty stupid. David knew this, and in the first four verses most theologians believe David is describing our relationship to God as sheep are with their shepherds. Most theologians then say David presents a different relationship in verse 5. Even the scripture notes in my Bible refer to this as in ancient Near Eastern culture, at a banquet it was customary to anoint a person with fragrant oil like a lotion. The hosts were also expected to protect their guests at all costs.

But Haddon Robinson has a different view and one that I personally like. It is based upon the lengthy study of shepherds of the Middle East by a Charles Slemming. That study revealed that before a shepherd lets his sheep into a new field to feast, that he checks the field out very closely, looking for bad grass and also vipers. These small poisonous snakes live in small holes in the ground and will come out and bite the nose of the sheep as they are grazing and kill them. Well, the shepherd finds the holes and pours some oil from his flask into it. This way the hole is too slippery for the vipers to crawl out. The shepherd also puts a small amount of oil on the head of each of the sheep. This acts as a repellant for the snakes in case the shepherd missed a few holes.

In the book of Matthew 10:16....Jesus said, "I send you forth as sheep in the midst of wolves." God knows that in life there will be dangers around us, like wrong friends, wrong music, wrong e-mail messages, etc., but with our trust in God as our Shepherd, then we can graze safely in dangerous pastures. You've learned here at camp or before you came here, that to float on water you have to learn to trust that the water will bear you up. After you've learned that the water will indeed bear you up, then you can float comfortably and easily. Well. If you haven't learned yet to trust the Shepherd to bear you up and make your life easier and more enjoyable, then get with me sometime while you're here at camp. To help remind you of today's thoughts, I've got some snakes to pass out to you right after our closing prayer.

CLOSING PRAYER

Reminder Item: Tiny plastic toy snakes

Associated Music:
  Note: The scouts really liked the snakes, but as a word of caution, remind the scouts not to use the snakes to frighten anyone. The first time I passed out the snakes, some scout (and I'm sure it was inadvertently-HA!) left his snake on the dining hall counter top where you pick up your tray of food. Shortly, a blood curdling scream was heard through out the campsite and a loud bang when the tray of food hit the floor. Thank goodness this was the last day of camp, because I heard that some Scoutmaster's wife was trying to run me down. And I don't think she was wanting to thank me. I think she literally or conscientiously wanted to run me down.

Title: Nuts

Opening Prayer

Scripture Reading: Old Testament, Proverbs 3:11-12 The purpose of the Book of Proverbs is to teach us how to obtain wisdom, and how to do what is right and just.

> *11/ My child, don't ignore it when God disciplines you or lets bad things happen to you. 12/ For God corrects those he loves, just as a father corrects a child he loves.*

New Testament, James 1:2-4 James, Jesus half-brother, explains here what Christians might expect and how to deal with it.

> *2/ Dear Brothers and Sisters, whenever trouble comes your way, let it be an opportunity for joy. 3/ For when your faith is tested, your endurance has a chance to grow. 4/ So let it grow, for when your endurance is fully developed, you will be strong in character and ready for anything.*

Question: Have you ever wondered why God lets you get sick, fail a test, or have a close friend move away?

Could it be that we're not taking life seriously enough unless something bad happens to us? Is it possible that the only way we get closer to God is to have to struggle now and then? I'm sure your Nature Merit Badge instructor can fill you in on some comparisons in nature and with rough times and growth.

You've seen pecans or walnuts I'm sure, and they have a pretty tough shell and it's hard to crack. Well, in the desert there are some seeds that have shells that are even harder than the pecan or walnut shells. The desert seeds' hard outer shell protects them from desert heat but it also prevents water from getting in. And if living water can't penetrate it, then it will never grow into the beautiful plant God wants it to be. But, when the heavy rains finally come every year or so, these seeds are carried along and banged against sand, gravel, and rocks. The shell of the seed is then scratched, nicked, and even cracked. And because of this, living water can now enter the shell. And the seed can now begin to grow. Grow into the beautiful plant God intended.

In a similar way, the hurts and pains that sometimes bang into us are just what we need to let God's love and power to get into us. Often we just take life for granted and totally forget about God. But when trouble hits, we soon realize again that we need to turn to God for help. So the nicks and scratches that come along (and you might even get some here at camp this week) should help us open ourselves up to God and let Him in, into our lives. It's God's way of helping us grow.

I've got something to pass out right after the closing prayer to help you remember what we've talked about today. You know, after we've been nicked and scratched, and we open ourselves up to God, things are just a lot better, life is a lot sweeter...kind of like this Snickers bar.

Closing Prayer

Reminder Item: I've used miniature Snicker bars (or any candy with nuts in it) or I've passed out pecans in the shell

Associated Music:

Title: Bowling with Roly-Polies

Opening Prayer

Scripture Reading: Old Testament, Psalm 91:4

> He will shield you with his wings. He will shelter you with his feathers. His faithful promises are your armor and protection.

New Testament, Ephesians 6:11-12 Paul wrote this letter to the believers in Ephesus to strengthen and encourage them.

> 11/ Put on all of God's armor so that you will be able to stand firm against all strategies and tricks of the Devil. 12/ For we are not fighting against people made of flesh and blood, but against the evil rulers of the unseen world....

Fact: You know- God doesn't promise a world free from danger, but He does promise His help whenever we face danger.

Question: Is everyone here familiar with a Roly-Poly? Maybe some of you call them pill bugs. Can anyone tell me if they are an insect or a bug?

How many of you have tasted lobster? How many of you like to eat lobster? How many of you have eaten a roly-poly? Well, most people would think that is pretty gross. You think of the roly-poly as being an insect or bug, but really it is a member of the crustacean family, the same family as the lobster or shrimp. So, in a sense, if you boiled maybe 3000 roly-polies you'd have a meal equivalent to a lobster dinner. The roly-poly, like the rest of the crustacean family breathes through gills that are located in its feet, so the feet must be kept moist in order for it to breathe. That's why you will find roly-polies under rocks or wherever there is some moisture. You get them out of their moist habitat and they will not live very long.

The roly-poly also has some similarities to the armadillo, it carries its' defensive shelter with it wherever it goes. They both have a shield of armor that is in segments and whenever they feel threatened they roll up inside that shield of armor that becomes like a round ball and they are protected from all sides.

Now I had a couple of pet armadillos for a short time when I was younger. I couldn't call them much of a pet though, because both the armadillo and the roly-poly are nocturnal. They only come out at night, the rest of the time they are rolled up in a ball in their protective shield of armor. Now I never went bowling with an armadillo, but I have with a roly-poly. Two or more of my buddies would get a roly-poly and we would roll our roly-poly to see who's rolled the farthest.

The scripture today mentions a shield of armor that we can have with us at all times. The Armor of God. Why should we carry God's armor with us? All the time we're being hit with views and thoughts of sin through people, television, some movies and music, and even more so today by the internet by pop-ups or e-mails. We must have God's armor to help us with the truth, to protect us from falling prey or into a trap that is not good for us.

The things you are learning here at camp are helping you become knowledgeable about the world and how to survive, but we still always need God's armor.

Today, to help remind you of God's armor, we've got a smooth grey rock (similar to a large roly-poly). Carry it in your pocket to help remind you of this message and to remember to carry God's armor with you.

Closing Prayer

Reminder Item: I've used smooth round decorative rocks that come in a bag. Or you can buy some black marbles or balls that are inexpensive.

Associated Music:

Title: Meek Horses (Birdstoned)

Note: I first used this message in 2003 when a horse named FunnyCide was expected to win the coveted Triple-Crown at Belmont, after winning both the Kentucky Derby and the Preakness. A horse named EmpireMaker won the race, upsetting FunnyCide. This made it the 16th time that a horse that had already won both the Kentucky Derby and the Preakness failed to win the Belmont and the Triple-Crown. In 2004, I used the same message again, but was able to update the information because the same incident occurred again the next year.

Opening Prayer

Question:How many of you are taking the Horsemanship Merit Badge while here at camp? Well, today I'm going to tell you something else about some horses you probably don't know.

Scripture Reading:Psalm 37:11

> *Those who are gentle and lowly will possess the land; they will live in prosperous security.*

Matthew 5:5

> *Blessed (or happy) are the meek, for they will inherit the earth (or they will be the winners).*

Matthew 5:5 is the 5th Beatitude. The beatitudes are from Jesus Sermon on the Mount and are lessons for us from Jesus.

Around Jesus time the people had a different understanding of many of the words we hear and use today. One of these words is the word meek. What does the word meek mean to you? Weak? Mild-mannered? Gentle? Lowly?

Well, in Biblical times the word meek often referred to the winning horse in a horse race. The meek horse was a horse that submitted or listened to the rider or master. The horse submitted to the whip and to the leadership of the master. The horse was not weak because it was usually the first one out of the gate and the first one to lead the pack.

So, in the beatitudes and in the psalms we are told when we submit or listen to God and obey His Leadership then we will be happy and secure in knowing that we will inherit the earth, that we will be the ultimate winners, that we will be happy forever.

Recently, about four weeks ago, the Belmont Horse Race was held and the expected winner was to be a little red chestnut horse named SmartyJones. SmartyJones had already won two of America's most important horse races- the Kentucky Derby and the Preakness. He was expected to win the Belmont, too, making him a Triple-Crown winner. The first time in 31 years. But something happened. SmartyJones broke from the gates cleanly and moved right to the lead. But on the backstretch the jockey on BirdStone (the winning horse) noticed that SmartyJones was not listening or obeying his jockey (or master). The jockey (Stewart) wanted SmartyJones to relax and save some energy for the end of the race…but SmartyJones was fighting and not listening to his jockey. The other jockey knew right then he could win. His horse, BirdStone, was relaxed and obeying. The Meeker horse won again, Do you want to win?? Then, listen and obey God.

Right after our closing prayer I have a meek horse to pass out to each of you to help you remember that you can be a winner too by listening to God.

Closing Prayer

Reminder Item: a Plastic 2 ½" horse

Associated Music:

Title: Salty and Sweet

Opening Prayer

Statement: Today we'll hear what Jesus teaches us about being disciples. In all three scripture verses Jesus is telling us to be like good salt.

Scripture Reading: New Testament Matthew 5:13

> *You are the salt of the earth. But what good is salt if it has lost its flavor? Can you make it useful again? It will be thrown out and trampled underfoot as worthless.*

New Testament, Mark 9:50

> *Salt is good for seasoning. But if it loses its flavor, how do you make it salty again? You must have the qualities of salt among yourselves and live in peace with each other.*

New Testament, Luke 14:34

> *Salt is good for seasoning. But if it loses its flavor, how do you make it salty again? Flavorless salt is good neither for the soil nor for fertilizer. It is thrown away.*

What country is the world's largest producer of salt? The United States! And what two states are the biggest producers of salt? Louisiana and Texas. During Jesus time salt was highly valued and even used as money. Roman soldiers were even paid partly in salt. As a matter of fact the word 'salary' comes from the Latin word 'Salarium', which means 'Salt Money'.

    What does salt do? There are different kinds of salt. Rock Salt- This salt has dirt and other things in it. It has not been purified or refined but it can still be used to make ice cream or put on sidewalks to melt the ice. When we say 'Rock' Salt, that is exactly what salt is in its natural state. Salt is a rock crystal called "Halite" (Hay-lite). It is made of two different elements, sodium and chlorine. FYI, salt is the only rock we can eat. Of course before we can eat it, it has to be refined into tiny crystals. Does someone want to make a guess on how much salt the average person eats in a lifetime? Well, its 402 pounds. That's a pretty big rock.

Besides rock salt, there is Canning Salt. This is used for canning and preserving. It is pure, but it has no additives like iodine or aluminum. When Jesus says that we must have the qualities or preservatives, of salt. He is saying that we need to live among society and to permeate society with the love and message of God to help keep society from spoiling, or going bad, by moral decay or sin.

Then there is Table Salt, this is the best salt for adding flavor. But if this salt gets wet and dries, then it is no good. It cannot add flavor then and so it has no value. IF you and I as Christians and Believers in Christ make no affect on the world around us, then we are of little good or value to God. Instead, we need to affect others positively and make sure others know Jesus too. Then we are like the good salt that brings out the best in food.

As Christians, we are to preserve the good in the world and bring new flavor to life. Today, to help remind you of what Jesus expects of you….I've got some Salt Money.

CLOSING PRAYER

Reminder Item: Little packets of salt that you can get free from Fast Food Restaurants like McDonald's. There is also a small snack packet called 'Salty and Sweet' which contains salted peanuts, and chocolate candies mixed together, you can pass out as well.

Props: You can find examples of Rock Salt, Canning Salt, and Table Salt at your local grocery store.

Associated Music:

Title: God's the Real Thing

Opening Statement: "Today we'll learn about 'Living Water'."

Opening Prayer

Scripture Reading: Old Testament, Jeremiah 2:13

> *God says, "You have turned away from me- Me/God-the fountain of living water".*

We often elect to turn to money, to cars, or boats or other material things…. just to make our lives happy and good. But these things only temporarily please or refresh us. God promises to constantly refresh us with living water.

New Testament, John 4:13…Jesus is talking to the woman at the well who was getting well water for herself and Jesus offered her Living Water. Jesus said:

> *"People soon become thirsty again after drinking this water. But the water I give them takes away thirst altogether. It becomes a perpetual spring within them, giving them eternal life."*

I've got a few slogans today to help you remember God. Some of these will sound familiar to you…. Can you tell me what advertisement this sounds like?

1. A day without God is like a day without sunshine. (orange juice commercial)
2. God can double your pleasure and double your fun. (double mint gum)
3. Don't leave home without Him. (American Express)
4. God's the real thing. (CocaCola)
5. You're in Good Hands with God. (Allstate Insurance)
6. (the adult leaders might recognize this one) When you say God, you've said it all? (Budweiser)
And on Prayer…
7. Prayer is 'The Pause that Refreshes' (CocaCola)

Sometimes our lives, and maybe even here at camp this week, we will have problems that will shake us up. And we'll get so shook up on the inside that we'll just about explode. Kind of like this can of coke. When it gets shook up, what is going to happen with it when we finally open it. IT E-X-P-L-O-D-E-S!

Did you know that coke is 99% colored sugar water? So it only takes a little bit of the other ingredients to make it explode. What can we do with this can of pop now to keep it from exploding?? Let it sit for a while and let it calm down-Right?

And for us? When some little thing is about to make us explode.. We need to turn to GOD 'He's the Real Thing' and then take a little time for prayer. And that pause will refresh us! Then we won't explode either-just like this can of pop won't explode. Okay-Did you get the message? Let's close in prayer, then I've got something for you to help you remember this message today. Alright, everyone gets a can of pop today. But I don't want to hear of any exploding pop, okay? And then, what are you going to do with the empty cans?

Closing Prayer

Reminder Item: In this case, I was able to buy some Wal-mart pop in the small 6oz cans. This pop gave me the opportunity to ask the scouts if this pop was the "the Real Thing" and again remind them that God IS the Real Thing.

Prop: You buy a can of Coke and drill a small inconspicuous hole in it. You drain the coke out and fill it back up with water. You then hold your finger over the hole while you shake the can up. Then when you pop the tab right in front of the scouts, nothing happens. It doesn't explode and you can just pour the liquid out.

Associated Music: U2 "Even Better Than The Real Thing", and Toby Mac "No One Like You"

Title: GOD'S WAVE

Opening Prayer

Scripture Reading: Old Testament, Hebrews 2:1

> *So we must listen very carefully or we may drift away.*

(Like in FM Broadcasting- FM receivers may tend to drift from the frequency to which they are tuned and will no longer pick up the sender). FM=Frequency Modulation/AM=Amplitude

New Testament, Mark 4:9

> *Anyone who is willing to hear should listen and understand.*

I have this FM radio on right now, and the volume is up, but I can't hear anything. What could my problem be? I'm not tuned in clearly? I'm not on a broadcasting frequency? The antenna is broken?

You know, at any given time, there may be millions of signals in the air bouncing around us. Right now as you sit here-there are signals carrying messages of music, people talking, and even pictures coming in from different senders and stations. TV stations, walkie-talkies, radios, and cellular phones. If you could pick up and hear all those signals at the same time, the noise and the sounds would drive us crazy. But God spared us of this.

Now there are certain sounds that we can't pick up, but animals, birds, and fish can. Today, with some technological help, we too can pick up some of these sounds. Do you think? Do you think? That God and Angels may be speaking to us too and that we just aren't tuned in? Could that be? Maybe you know someone or have heard stories of people who said they heard a voice from someone who warned them of something. Or the voice told them what to do. Many times in the Bible we read of people hearing God's voice and telling them what to do.

As we grow and learn more about God, our ears and brain are more tuned in to Him and to what He is saying to us. And it might not be His voice we hear- maybe He put His words into the voice of a friend or even a total stranger who offers us words of encouragement or love or caring. Maybe it's not His voice, but His majestic glory, His stunning creations that will speak to us. Get tuned in to Him here at camp with all His beauty that surrounds you, the hills, the trees, the birds, the insects, the stars, the sounds.

So my message today is to take a little time each day and pray, be silent, then listen and observe and hear and understand what God is saying to you. Just as this radio can be adjusted and tuned in to certain Radio waves-let us become adjusted and tuned in to God's Wave.

CLOSING PRAYER

Reminder Item: small racing flag pins

Props: a portable radio. At first have it set where it can't pick up anything except maybe static. Then as you tune it in, you'll pick up a station clearly.

Associated Music: Toby Mac with Diverse City- 'Hey Now'
DC Talk 'Atmosphere'

Chapter Five

TITLE: THE KEY

OPENING PRAYER

Scripture Reading: New Testament, Matthew 16:19

> *Jesus says, "I will give you the keys of the kingdom of Heaven."*

New Testament, Revelation 1:17

> *Jesus says, "I hold the keys of death and the grave."*

As believers in Jesus, we don't have to fear death or the grave because Jesus holds the keys to both.

This morning I want to fill you in on what took years for me to figure out. In just a minute I'm going to ask you a couple of questions that I've asked a lot of people-mostly High School youth at my church in Tulsa. Some people answer the questions one way and some another way- some say they're not sure and some say they don't know. Now, when I'm talking to 2 or 3 youth at one time-they can answer me directly. But there are too many of you here this morning- so you'll just answer the question in your mind-in silence.

Something happened in my scout troop a couple of years ago that concerned me. A couple of our sharpest Eagle Scouts lost their lives in separate auto accidents within one year. It made me realize that we never know when our last day on earth may be-even if we are a young Eagle Scout. We just never know. Here's my first question to you. Do you know for sure, without a doubt, without any question in your mind, without any reservation whatsoever, that you are going to have eternal life? Now, some of you may be thinking, I know without a doubt, or you might be thinking I think I do, or maybe I'm not sure. I get these different answers all the time. Now, my second question is and particularly for those of you who said you are sure you are going to have eternal life…Why do you know you're going to have eternal life? What if something happened to you tomorrow and you go to Heaven and God meets you there and asks you… "Why should I let you into Heaven?" I get all sorts of answers for this question too, but now I'm going to tell you the answer to both of the questions, just as simple as I can.

(Holding up a BSA Skiing Book) Do you see this book: What do you think this book is going to tell you? How to Ski? Right! It's pretty plain isn't it? It's right here on the cover. (Holding up a Bible) What is this book going to tell you? A little harder-not so plain is it. A song came out a few years ago by a Christian group called 'Burlap to Cashmere' and the title of their song was "B-I-B-L-E, (Basic Instructions Before Leaving Earth). If that were written on this cover it would entice more of us to pick it up and read it probably. There is also one sentence in the Bible in 1st John 5:13, where John tells us,

> *"These words (or this Book) is written, so that you may know you have eternal life".*

Now in this book (BSA Skiing book), what do you think the Key thing is that you need to go skiing? Skis right? Now you can go skiing without even reading this book, so long as you have skis. You might find it's a little bumpy, kind of tough though. You could take the ski lift up to the top of the mountain and you can look down and see that big, big Lodge with lots and lots of rooms at the end of the ski trail. You know its' nice and warm there. Your friends are all there. Some hot chocolate is there, and all that good stuff. And you know what? You'll get there all right because you've got the key thing you need, the skis. Oh sure it will be a little bumpy, kind of tough, you'll take a few falls, BUT you will get there. Let me tell you what the Key is in this Book, in John 6:47-Jesus says,

> *"If you know me, if you believe in me, you'll have eternal life".*
> He's the key. That is all there is to it. You don't have to read the Bible, you don't have to do this or do that. BUT, in this book (ski book) or this Book (Bible)… if you read it, or if you listen to some good instructors or teachers or guides… Guess what? Your trip will be a whole lot smoother. Did what I just say, sink in to you for the first time in your life? If it did, I'd like for you to tell me sometime before you leave camp. I'd like to know and I'd like to encourage you.

I've got something for all of you to take with you today to help you remember today's message. You can pick one up right after our closing prayer. And thank you for being here today.

Closing Prayer

Reminder Item: I was able to get 300-400 keys from local key shops for free. These were old used keys that were no longer any good.

Associated Music: "Big House" by Audio Adrenaline and "B.I.B.L.E." by Burlap to Cashmere

Title: PHOS CROSS

Opening Prayer

Scripture Reading: Old Testament, Psalm 18:28

> *Lord, you have brought light into my life; my God, you light up my darkness.*

New Testament, John 8:12

> *Jesus said to the people, "I am the light of the world. If you follow me, you won't be stumbling through the darkness..."*

One of the songs you heard this morning is one of the oldest (if not the oldest) hymns known. The hymn in Greek is called 'Phos Hilaron' which means joyful light. Hilaron=joyful or hilarious/ Phos=light

This song is almost 2000 years old. First records of it date not long after Jesus' crucifixion. It was sung in the evening at the tomb of Jesus in Jerusalem as a permanently lit candle was brought from the tomb. The hymn symbolized the Light of Jesus and the Joy of His Resurrection.

I've got a cross here that's called a Phos Cross because it has the capacity to glow or give light in the dark. Inside this cross is phosphorous, and when you hold it close to a light it will glow. The longer you hold it near the light, and the closer you get it to the light, the brighter and longer it will glow. Did you know that our body has phosphorous in it too? It is one of the six key elements that make up our body. If you weigh 100 pounds, then you'll have a whole pound of phosphorous in you. Our supply of phosphorous comes from things we eat. Look at a milk carton or a box of cereal or even potato chips for instance and you'll see that phosphorous is one of the ingredients. Maybe you've heard people say of someone: "that person has a special glow about them."

In Exodus 34:29, when Moses spoke to God up on the Sinai Mountain top and wrote the Ten Commandments....**His face glowed after spending time with God.** And in Exodus 34:34-35, whenever Moses went to speak with God, **the people would see his face aglow**. Do you suppose? Do you suppose? That while this cross gets its strength and source of power from light…that maybe you and I get our strength and our glow from being close to Jesus/God and spending time and staying close to Him as much as we can? If so, then we will glow and we can be a light for others, and people will know that we have been with God.

After the Closing Prayer, everyone can have one of these 'glowing Crosses'.

Closing Prayer

Reminder Item: A Glo-Cross Necklace.

Associated Music: 'Phos Hilaron'
'Joyous Light'

Phos Hilaron
(Hail Gladdening Light)

1.
Hail Gladdening Light
Of His pure glory poured
Who is the Immortal Father, Heavenly Blest
Holiest of Holies, Jesus Christ our Lord

2.
Now we are come to the sun's hour of rest
The lights of evening 'round us shine
We hymn the Father, Son, and Holy Spirit Divine

3.
Worthiest art Thou, at all times to be sung
With undefiled tongue
Son of our God, Giver of life alone
Therefore, in all the world Thy glories Lord
Thine own

Track produced by Steve Fee
Programming and additional production by Josh Hailey
© 2004 worship together.com Songs/six steps Music / ASCAP / Admin. By EMI Christian Music Publishing

Joyous Light
(Hail Gladdening Light-Revised)

1.
Hail Gladdening Light, sun so bright
Jesus Christ, end of night, alleluia
Hail Gladdening Light, Eternal Bright
In evening time, 'round us shine, alleluia, alleluia

2.
Hail Gladdening Light, such joyous Light
O Brilliant Star, forever shine, alleluia, alleluia

We hymn the Father, we hymn the Son
We hymn the Spirit, wholly Divine
No one more worthy of songs to be sung
To the Giver of Life, all glory is Thine

Chris Tomlin: Acoustic Guitar and Vocals

Daniel Carson: Electric Guitar

Jesse Reeves: Bass

Joey Parish: Drums

Arrangement and additional chorus by Chris Tomlin and David Crowder

©2004 worship together.com Songs / six steps Music/ ASCAP / Admin. By EMI Christian Music Publishing

Title: TANDEM BICYCLE

Opening Prayer

Scripture Reading: Old Testament, Psalm 145:18-19

> *18/ The Lord is close to all who call on Him, yes to all who call on Him sincerely. 19/ He fulfills the desires of those who fear him: He hears their cries for help and rescues them.*

New Testament, Romans 12:8 Paul in this letter is telling the Believers in Rome how to live out their faith….

> *8/ If God has given you leadership ability, take the responsibility seriously.*

This morning we're going to talk about winning the Race (The Race of life). Winning a long race can be great…but if getting there means struggle and pain and grief, it can be rough. If we have God with us on our journey though, we can have joy along the way. (This is talked about in Psalm 84).

One of the Merit Badges you can earn here at camp is the 'Mountain Biking' Badge. My story today has to do with Bicycling. Who knows what a tandem bicycle is? (2 seats and 2 sets of pedals) I'm going to talk about a bike race which in reality could be your race in life. Let's say you hear about a bike race across the country with a Big Cash Prize for the winner. Well, you feel pretty confident because you've gotten your Scout Merit Badge in Mountain Biking, Personal Fitness, and Orienteering. But this is a tandem race and you have to have a racing buddy. You feel you don't need anyone, but someone tells you about ABBA. (This is Aramaic for father or God as referred to in The Book). Since you don't know how good ABBA is, you tell him to take the back seat. You know the way, you've got the strength, so you tell ABBA you'll take the front seat and you'll take us both to the finish line

Things start out great, it's a great day, the birds are singing, the weather is perfect. You have a slight downhill grade, then some flat roads. But soon you come to a fork in the road and you have to guess which way to go. You decide to go to the left. Well, after a long ways, it turns into a Dead End. You have to go back and get on the right road. Then its going pretty smooth again and you hear the birds singing. But then the paved road ends and you hit some dirt roads and some ruts and it gets bumpy. Soon, though you get back on a smooth and level road, but then you come upon the desert and it starts getting hot. ABBA is sitting back there letting you do all the work. Then up ahead you see the mountains. Soon it's all uphill and you're exhausted. Finally, you turn to ABBA and ask Him for His help. So you change seats and let ABBA take control. Now, you're finally sitting back relaxing and taking in the view and listening to the birds sing along the way. How much better the race is now. You realize then that you should have let ABBA have the front seat a long time ago. Sometimes we need to turn to God for help before we're just worn out and exhausted.

CLOSING PRAYER….

Today God, we pray that in the future we will call on you more and more to lead the way. To sit on the front seat of our tandem bicycle so that we can see the beauty around us; and hear the birds singing along the way. Amen

Today, to help you remember to enjoy life's journey, we've got a song bird for all of you. Have a Great Day!

Reminder Item: water-filled song bird

Prop: Hand out a half-dozen song birds filled with water to some of the early arrivals. Explain how the bird works and tell them whenever they hear me say 'The Birds are Singing' in the message, to start making the bird sing.

Associated Music: Delirious 'The Happy Song'

Title: MONKEY SEE-MONKEY DO

Opening Prayer

Scripture Reading: Old Testament, 1ˢᵗ Kings 10:22

> *The king had a fleet of trading ships that sailed with Hiram's fleet. Once every three years the ships returned, loaded down with gold, silver, ivory, apes, and peacocks.*

Old Testament, Proverbs 3:31

> *"Do not envy violent people: don't copy their ways"*

FACT: Monkeys were not common in the lands ruled by the Kings in the Bible, so they were imported along with gold, silver, and ivory from nations like India or Africa. Some Bible translations (including my New Living Bible) refer to monkeys and baboons as 'Peacocks'. Why, I'm not sure, but maybe it had something to do with a baboon's bare buttocks. Once a month, when the female goes into heat, her rump or buttock changes color from grey to pink.

The cliché or acronym (or old saying) of "Monkey See, Monkey Do" comes from a monkey watching and copying an action by someone or something else. We do that too, and if we're not careful we'll copy and do the wrong thing, as monkeys often do.

I need a couple of scouts who like bananas to come up front for a minute. I'd like them to have a banana to eat. Now, show us how you're going to open and peel and eat this banana.

OBSERVE AND COMMENT: In most cases, everyone peels the banana from the stem. Then describe how, if you observe a monkey, the monkeys open and peel a banana. It's much easier the way a monkey does it. A monkey peels the banana from the opposite end, the end from which the flower blossom grows from the banana plant. Bananas come from a plant and not a tree as we always describe them. The plant grows about 8 to 10 feet high and has bunches of bananas that grow up instead of hanging down, which is the way we picture them. A bunch may be as high as 6 feet and weigh around 100 to 150 pounds. So, it is much easier for the monkey to peel a banana from the flowering end. If you've ever tried to peel a green banana from the stalk end, you'll find it very difficult. BUT, peeling it from the opposite end is always easier.

So why do we peel a banana from the stalk end? Because, we've seen everybody else do it that way. We've never questioned if it was the right way or not. In our lives, we might see a lot of people doing things that are wrong and we might just copy it ourselves, UNLESS, someone who knows the right way instructs us in the right way. Some people, some music, some movies, some TV shows, some stuff we see on our computers can lead us in the wrong direction. Before you let this happen, or if you think it might be wrong, READ the Book of Proverbs in your Bible. Let me read to you the very first part of Proverbs…..Chapter 1 verses 2 through 6:

> *2/ "The purpose of these proverbs is to teach people wisdom and discipline, and to help them understand wise sayings. 3/ Through these proverbs, people will receive instruction in discipline, good conduct, and doing what is right, just, and fair. 4/ These proverbs will make the simple-minded clever. They will give knowledge and purpose to young people. 5/ Let those who are wise listen to these proverbs and become even wiser. And let those who understand receive guidance 6/ by exploring the depth of meaning in these proverbs, parables, wise sayings, and riddles."*

You know, there are 31 chapters in the Book of Proverbs…You would be very wise to read a Chapter a day for the next 31 days. Proverbs 2:20 says:

> *"Follow the steps of good men, and stay on the paths of the righteous."* So, I'm saying, watch and copy your Scout Leaders and the staff here at camp. And be wise in what you copy. And, if a leader or staffer is not wise, then instruct them and tell them, and if they are wise, they will love you all the more.

Favorite Devotions   81

Now who said this?

"A bowl of soup with someone you love, is better than steak with someone you hate."

Let me say that again…..OK, now everyone say it with me…All Right! You guys just learned a verse of scripture by King Soloman (Proverbs 15:17 NLT). Now, let me read this scripture to you from the King James Version of the Bible...*Better is a dinner of herbs where love is, than a stalled ox and hatred therewith.* And in the Revised Standard Version it says....*Better is a dinner of herbs where love is than a fatted ox and hatred with it.* It is hard to understand what these last two Bibles are saying in these verses isn't it. So find a Bible that you can understand. Words and meanings change over the years and so Bibles need to be updated every now and then. I read the King James Version from front to back right after college and it just didn't make any sense to me then and I still have a hard time with it now.

Now, there is a deeper meaning to this scripture than what we first see… *"A bowl of soup with someone you love, is better than steak with someone you hate."* We'll not go into it here, but back at your camp site this evening you may want to dig deeper into it.

CLOSING PRAYER

Reminder Item: Some dried banana chips, tiny plastic monkeys, or whole bananas (which you can buy by the box at $0.25/ lb, this figures to be about $0.05 to $0.08 a banana)

Associated Music:

Chapter Five

TITLE: ALARM CLOCK

OPENING PRAYER

Scripture Reading: Old Testament, Exodus 16:23

> "The Lord has appointed a day of rest, a holy Sabbath to the Lord. On this day we will rest from our normal daily tasks."

New Testament, Mark 6:31

> Then Jesus said, "Let's get away from the crowds for a while and rest."

I've got some time on my hands this morning and I want to spend a little time talking about time.

Here's a riddle for you. Do you know what a clock does when it's still hungry? It goes back four seconds!

Did some of you have a hard time getting up this morning? If you did, then maybe you didn't get enough rest last night.

The Bible talks about the importance of rest and getting enough of it. And it tells us about taking some time out in our daily routine to spend time in the understanding of God and in the worship of God. If you do not get enough rest at night you cannot be an effective learner. At school, at church, here at Scout Camp- your teachers, your youth ministers, the staff here at camp have something to teach you that you will benefit from. But if you're day dreaming, or your brain is running on slow speed, or you're completely dozing off, you just can't learn.

Now the Bible isn't telling you, and I'm not telling you to take some Extra Slumber. But figure out how much rest you do need. If you're falling asleep during classes then you need some more sleep. Studies show that most school kids need 9 hours of sleep to keep healthy and alert. Maybe *you* can get by on less, but figure it out.

The clock industry makes a variety of alarm clocks, because different people need different ways of being awakened. If you're getting enough rest, a nice gentle alarm may wake you up. Some of you might need a BIG BEN type of alarm that clangs and clangs. Some of you may prefer an alarm that gives you a reason for getting up. A fishing alarm or a golf alarm that tells you its time to get up and go fishing or golfing. You know, I'd like an alarm that says. "Good Morning! This is God speaking. It's time for you to get up. I'm here to make your day. So take some time to pray before you get away!"

Wouldn't it be nice to have a reminder every day that God is going to be with us all day, every day.

Well I thank all of you for coming to Chapel this morning and I hope all of you got enough rest last night so you were able to understand today's message.

Closing Prayer

Reminder Item: Mini-bugle or trumpet to symbolize a wake-up call

Props: some different alarm clocks

Associated Music:

Title: CRASH

Opening Prayer

Scripture Reading: New Testament, 2nd Corinthians 1:4

> *God comforts us in all of our troubles so that we can comfort others. When others are troubled, we will be able to give them the same comfort God has given us.*

We need to remember that every trial or problem that we may endure should give us the strength and the passion to comfort and help other people who are suffering similar problems.

About six months after Hurricane Katrina had crashed into New Orleans and other parts of the Gulf, on August 29, 2005, I got to go there on a working Mission trip. Our team flew into the airport, and the airport had just received more damage from a tornado just a couple of days before we arrived. Driving into the city on the highway from the airport, it really looked like things were getting back to normal. Oh yeah! We saw a lot of houses with blue tarps on the roof, but from the highway you could see cars parked in the streets and driveways so we figured people had started moving back. But, that afternoon when we were assigned our first house to gut out, we realized all those cars we saw were abandoned, and the houses were deserted. There was no water, no electricity, and no gas. It gave you a very strange feeling. I don't know how many of you are familiar with the series of books and the movie called 'Left Behind', but that was the kind of feeling several of us got. We felt like God had called the ones who believed in Him and left the rest of us behind.

There were miles upon miles of deserted homes and thousands upon thousands of abandoned vehicles. Most of our team had experienced some problems of our own in life, which we were able to get through with the help of God. So now we felt we should help others during their time of suffering. Helping them physically and spiritually. We were able to help three families in the 4 days we were there. Lots and lots of other people and teams are going there to help also, but it may still take 10 to 15 years to recover.

When you have problems come crashing into your lives, whether here at camp or sometime in the future, remember to turn to God for help. And then remember to help others down the road that are having similar problems.

2nd Scripture Reading: New Testament, John 7:13

> But no one had the courage to speak favorably about Him in public, for they were afraid of getting in trouble with the Jewish leaders.

Although many people talk about Christ in Church, when it comes to making a public statement about their faith, they are often afraid.

Now I've got a little quiz called 'Animal Group Names'.
If I say:
    A group of sheep are called a 'Flock'
    Or a bunch of cattle are called a 'Herd'
Then what do you call:
    A group of dogs? A 'Pack'
    What about a group of monkeys? A 'Barrel'

The next few may not be as familiar to you, but they make sense.
What do you call:
    A group of rattlesnakes? A 'Rumba'
    A group of giraffes? A 'Tower'
    A group of baboons? A 'Troop'
    A group of eagles? A 'Convocation'

Now, let me define convocation. In the Bible where it is mentioned, it means a holy gathering. Or it means a gathering of important people. Like a convocation of Senators, or maybe we could say a convocation of Eagle Scouts.

Okay, I'm leading up to the last group name.

What is the group name for Rhinoceroses? Well, a group of Rhinos is called: A 'Crash'. How did they acquire this name? Some Rhinos can weigh as much as elephants. Some weigh up to 4 tons. But even with their great size and weight they are still pretty fast on their feet. In a charge they can get up to 25-30 mph. The dangerous thing is that they can't stop very fast and they have another problem. They have weak eyes and they can't see very far. So they often CRASH into something before they can stop. But it is said that a rhino has no fear of crashing.

You know, I think God would like us to be like a rhino for Him. Just charge out, with no fear whatsoever, and tell others about Him. Our last scripture talked about people being afraid to tell others about Him. God wants us not to be afraid, but to be more like the rhino.

Closing Prayer

Reminder Item: Plastic Jungle Animals about 5 cents each.

Associated Music: 'Here Am I' by Mercy Me

Title: Reveille & Revelation

Opening Prayer

Scripture Reading: Old Testament, Psalm 17:15

> *But because I have done what is right, I will see you when I awake.*
> *I will be fully satisfied, for I will see you face to face.*

Is there someone here who would like to define the word Reveille? Simply, it means 'to awaken'. It's a signal for soldiers, or in our case here at Camp Tom Hale, for the troops to wake up. It is usually done with a bugle or drum.

New Testament, Matthew 11:27

> *No one really knows the Son except the Father, and no one really knows the Father except the Son, and those to whom the son chooses to reveal.*

Okay, Revelation. What do you think it might mean? What about Reveal? It is to make something known. And Revelation means a 'revealing'. In theology, Revelation is God making Himself known.

On the song sheet I passed out this morning are a couple of songs where the artist is trying to awaken you and reveal God to you. I purposely did not tell you who the artists are and I hope you can tell me. I played 'Better is One Day' earlier. Now, I'm going to play 'Beautiful Day'. Use the song sheet to follow along with the music. [Play the song... 'Beautiful Day']

Now, who can tell me who the lead singer is in the song and the name of the group? It's Bono and U2. Who wants to make a guess to who the artist was in the fist song, 'Better is One Day'? It's Matt Redman. Now, look at the words to his song while I read some verses from Psalm 84. 84:1-2

> *How lovely is your dwelling place, O Lord Almighty. I long, yes, I faint with longing to enter the courts of the Lord. And then verse 84:10 A single day in your courts is better than a thousand*

anywhere else! Redman's song is right from this Psalm. And the Psalms are a collection of songs.

Matt Redman is from Watford, England and his music is heard only on Christian radio stations. His songs are popular all over the world, particularly with college groups and churches. Bono and U2 are from Ireland and their music is usually heard only on Rock Music stations. They are popular all over the world and many of their fans are non-churched.

Both of these popular artists are strong Christians. As a matter of fact, Bono was the featured speaker at the February 2006 National Prayer Breakfast in Washington, DC. Bono is considered to be a Radical for Jesus, but most of his fans do not realize this. If you know your Bible you can see where and what U2 is referring to in many of their songs. If you're not a churched person and not familiar with the Bible then you will not see the real message that U2 is revealing. Take a song sheet with you and back at camp sometime, see if you can find those parts of the song where U2 is referring to God and the Bible. Both of these gifted musicians want their listeners to wake up and know about God. They do it in different ways and they reach a different audience but they are waking a lot of young people up.

Closing Prayer

Reminder Item: Plastic Mini-Bugle for reveille or some type of musical instrument.

Associated Music: 'Better is One Day' Matt Redman
'Beautiful Day' U2

CHAPTER SIX

DEVOTION IDEAS AND HELPFUL SUGGESTIONS FROM OTHER HSR CHAPLAINS

Carl Amend (carlamend@sbcglobal.net) from Texas is going into his third year as a Chaplain at HSR. With a last name of Amend, how can you not be involved in serving the Lord in some aspect or another. Carl approached me on his first year at HSR with his scout troop and asked if he could play his bagpipe at one of the services. Carl is one of those people gifted musically. He will play a musical instrument or lead the scouts in praise and worship songs at his morning services.

One year he took a white board easel and wrote down letters and their meaning so that the scouts could better understand his lesson of the day. Examples…..

Bread of Life
    Box-Think outside the box
    Read-Read everyday

Eat-Good food that will feed your mind
Ask-Questions
Don't-Stop asking questions

Observe- Stop and smell the roses each day
Focus-On a task and stick with it

Learn- Something new everyday
Imagination- Don't lose your imagination
Finish- What you start…..
Enthusiasm- Is contagious

Reminder Item: After this lesson he passed out "mini-loaves" of bread that were actually sour dough pretzels, but they looked like a small loaf of bread.

Life Saver

    Look- for opportunities to do good
    I- can be a life saver
    Fellow Man- think of other's before yourself
    Everybody- needs a life saver

    S.O.S- who do you call when you need help?
    A friend- will last forever if the Lord is Lord of them…
    Value- your friendships, and they can and will last forever…
    Everybody- needs a friend
    Remember- to stay in touch with your friends

Reminder Item: Two wrapped lifesavers, one for the scout and one for them to give to a new found friend they met at camp.

Prop: A PFD (Personal Flotation Device), But also Protection From Danger. God is our PFD, He's our Papa, Friend, and Doesn't stop loving us.

Living Water

    Love- faith, hope, love; greatest of these is love

Improve- do something to better yourself every day...
Value- you have value, so do others...
Involve- others, make it a team effort
Nothing- is impossible with God
God's- way is always the best way...

Worship- is 24/7
Attitude- and versus
Teach- someone, who will teach someone else
Eternal- things we do today, have long-term consequences...
Remember- who is in control. God is in control...

Reminder Item and Props: Paper Dixie cup passed out. Mentally or physically paint a very hot/dry scene and ask scouts to drink from the dry cup. Then when leaving chapel have them fill their cups with cool refreshing water. Need some water jugs for this service.

Faith (You Gotta Have Faith....)
    Fall- down and get back up
    Assurance- confidence, stand firm
    Innocence- keep that child-like innocence
    Trust
    Hope

Reminder Items and Props: Hand out a dog biscuit, which actually looks like a civil war hard tack. Also hand out a Weetabix which looks like shredded wheat. Read out loud the natural and organic ingredients on both items. Then ask the scouts which one did they like better? Carl said some scouts came back and got another biscuit. The point being that this is an example of faith. They have faith in their mom's cooking, in restaurant food, and even the dining hall food at HSR.

Note: Carl makes copies of the songs to be sung and the scriptures he uses and passes them out.

Jonathan Reichman (jreichman@juno.com) from Tulsa is the person responsible for turning the chapel services around at Hale Scout Reservation. Through his dedication and determination and his reservoir of friends, he has made it a joy and pleasure to be a Chaplain of the week at HSR.

Jonathan provided some ideas about lessons for Chapel Services. He used the theme of "Treasurers" and used text from Proverbs 2 where it talks about seeking God's wisdom and understanding like one would seek after "silver and hidden treasure".

Still on the theme of "Treasures" he used II Corinthian 4, where Paul says that they did not use trickery or deceit, but declare the truth concerning Christ to them and then also use the verse

> *"we have this treasure in earthen vessels that the excellency of the power may be of God and not of man."* Jonathan points out that Christ in their lives was the treasure that Paul referred to.

Prop: A chenelle "pipe cleaner" was passed out and the scouts were asked to bring it back the next day in a shape that represents their relationship to God.

Jonathan suggests a lesson using the "Parable of the Purchased Field" from Matthews gospel. Another lesson comes from the Book of Revelation where it talks of God giving us a stone. And then giving the scouts a polished creek pebble as a reminder of God's promises received through Jesus Christ.

Another time Jonathan used and passed out a gospel tract written by Billy Graham, "Steps to Peace With God."

CHAPTER SEVEN

COMPILATION OF HELPFUL IDEAS AND SOURCES OF HANDOUTS

Here are some helpful hints and ideas gathered from my experiences and the experience of other Chaplains at Hale Scout Reservation. As you have already read, I come from a Christian background. I grew up in the Methodist denomination and then later in life I joined the Presbyterian denomination. Within both of these denominations, as well as most of the other denominations, you will find differences. For example, in the Presbyterian Churches, you will find some that are more traditional, some that are more contemporary, and some that are more evangelical. The music may be presented in a different manner. All may be Mission-oriented, but in different ways.

At HSR there are young people and adults there from maybe the same denomination, but with different backgrounds within their own denomination. There are also those coming to Chapel that are of different Christian denominations and also different religions. As Chaplains at HSR, we try to be sensitive and respectful to other Christian denominations and particular other religions. The arrival day of camp, we survey the troops in attendance to find out who we can expect in attendance at Chapel. AT HSR, we naturally expect a predominance of Christians. And, if that appears will be the case in attendance, then as a Christian Chaplain we can feel pretty comfortable and relaxed in doing Chapel according to our Christian background.

If it appears that youth of different Religious backgrounds may be attending, we thank the Scout Master and/or Adult leaders for letting us know and explain that we will work with them any way we can. If another time of day could be set to meet and gather with those young men, we will do it. If it is a matter of toning down the Good news of the New Testament, that can be done. In that case it may simply be a matter of Scripture Readings and Messages tying into the Old Testament and revising some of the music selected.

Getting the youth involved in Chapel Service is important. In many cases, a Troop has a young man who is a Chaplain Assistant and the Scout Master would like him involved or the young man himself would like to participate. Be sure to accommodate those particular requests. Some Chaplains are musically gifted and they can play musical instruments at Chapel. Some are song leaders and can get everyone involved in singing. Others, like me, can only play CD's. I have a preference for lively, contemporary Christian bands, and when Chapel is held the first thing in the morning, I've found the livelier and the louder the song is, the better received it is.

The reminder handouts are helpful and popular. Some people jokingly accuse us of bribing the Scouts to come to Chapel. But if it works, do it. Then the Scouts are starting out the day with an uplifting message. Many of the handouts that we have come up with are free or very inexpensive. If we plan carefully we can average an expense of around $20 a day at HSR. This is where attendance may average from 200-400 a day. Some of the free, or inexpensive items we have come up with are: Rocks, acorns, pop can tabs, used keys, pipe cleaners, pine cones, pine needles, rubber bands, shiny pennies, pecans, salt or sugar packets, toothpicks, paper clips, nails, etc. Most of these items you can find yourself or get free for the asking.

You can go to a local hobby store or a Christian book store and find all sorts of items sold in bulk that will figure out at five cents or less per item. You could check at a supply store or a Sam's Club store for items in bulk. Items like 'Tootsie Rolls' in bulk come to about two cents each or bags of the miniature candy bars run about five cents each. Also, if you plan ahead, you can order small items by the gross from a Toy Novelty Company like Kipp Bros. Inc. (www.kippbros.com) or Oriental Trading Co. (www.orientaltradingco.com) Some items we purchased from them before include: Glo-Cross Necklaces, Kazoos, Plastic Horses, Plastic Soldiers, Plastic Fish, Miniature Decks of Cards, and rubber snakes.

If you balance out some freebies with some purchased items, you can stay within a budget average of $20 a day. Carl Amend, the Chaplain from Texas, had a great idea of giving away a brand new, non-circulated Texas quarter on the last day of Chapel. He passed out little items the first four days that related to his messages and told them on Friday that they could trade any of those items in on a new Texas quarter.

Interesting Facts And Ideas To Point Out Upon Occasion

1) Today, with our modern technology such as computers, we're beginning to discover new messages that God concealed in the Bible. For instance:

The longest chapter in the Bible is Psalm 119 with 176 verses and the shortest chapter in the Bible is Psalm 117 with two verses. Between these two chapters would of course be Psalm 118. What has recently been discovered is that there are exactly 594 chapters before Psalm 118 and there are exactly 594 chapters after Psalm 118. If you add up all the chapters (594 plus 594), you get a total of 1188 chapters. And what is interesting is that Psalm 118, verse 8 (Psalm 118:8) is the center verse of the entire Bible. And what does this verse tell us? "It is better to trust the Lord than to put confidence in people."

Where are you putting your trust? Are you putting it in people or things? Our trust should be in God, who will guide us here on earth and on to our eternal destination.

2) Of the 12 Astronauts who have walked on the moon to date, eleven of them have been involved in Scouting.

3) On a plain piece of white paper put a black dot on it. Ask everybody what they see. Unfortunately almost everyone says they see a black dot. No one sees all the

white paper around the dot. Sometimes in our lives we will focus in on some minor thing (the black dot) and forget about all the good things (the white paper).

4) The Requirements of Faith in Jesus are:
   1. Knowing of Him
   2. Believing in Him
   3. Committing to Him

5) How can we make a difference for Jesus Christ?

We can tell someone we know about Him and ask them to tell someone they know. It's like geometric progression, take the example of a letter size piece of paper and fold it 50 times. If it could be done, each time you folded it, it would be twice as thick. So how high do you think it would be after you folded it 50 times? One foot? Three feet?, Ceiling height?

Actually, it would reach the sun. And if you were able to fold it one more time, it would reach the sun and back again. Can you tell someone about Jesus, and then have them tell someone they know?

6) Have you noticed what happens to a lump of hot charcoal when it falls off or away from the rest of the pile of charcoal?

It goes out doesn't it?

If you are a follower of Christ and on fire for Him, it is important for you to go to church and Sunday school and to hang around other believers. Otherwise, you will be like that piece of charcoal that falls away and the fire will go out of you.

7) Here is a quick and fun way that young people can learn their way through the Old and New Testament.

The Bible In 50 Words

God made

Adam bit

Noah arked

Abraham split

Jacob fooled

Joseph ruled
Bush talked
Moses balked
Pharaoh plagued
People walked
Sea divided
Tablets guided
Promise landed
Saul freaked
David peeked
Prophets warned

Jesus born
God walked
Love talked
Anger crucified
Hope died
Love rose
Spirit flamed
Word spread
God remained

8) This is a fun activity or game for the Scouts to do back at their campsite. There are 30 books of the Bible in this paragraph. Can you find them?

This is a most remarkable puzzle. A gentleman found it in an airplane seat pocket, on a flight from Los Angeles to Honolulu, keeping him occupied for hours. He enjoyed it so much; he passed it on to some friends. One friend from Illinois worked on this while fishing from his john boat. Another friend studied it while playing his banjo. Elaine Taylor, a columnist-friend, was so intrigued by it; she mentioned it in her weekly newspaper column. Another friend judges the job of solving this puzzle so involving, she brews a cup of tea to help her nerves. There will be some names that are really easy to spot. That's a fact. Some people, however, will soon find themselves in a jam; especially since the book names are not necessarily capitalized. Truthfully, from answers we get, we are forced to admit it usually takes a minister or scholar to see some of them at the worst. Research has shown that something in our genes is responsible for the difficulty we have in seeing the books in this paragraph. During a recent fund raising event, which featured this puzzle, the Alpha Delta Phi lemonade booth set a new sales record. The local paper, The Chronicle, surveyed over 200 patrons who reported that this puzzle was one of the most difficult they had ever seen. As Daniel Humana humbly puts it, "the books are all right there in plain view, hidden from sight." Those able to find all of them will hear great lamentations from those who have to be shown. One revelation that may help is that books like Timothy and Samuel may occur without their numbers. Also, keep in mind, that punctuation and spaces in the middle are normal. A chipper attitude will help you compete really well against those who claim to know the answers. Remember, there is no need for a mad exodus. There are really 30 books of the Bible lurking somewhere in this paragraph, waiting to be found.

9) This is also a fun thing to do at Chapel.
Here is a good way to get started off just before Chapel...

Tell everyone that God wants to make everyone feel a little better and that He wants them to get off to a good start today, BUT He is going to need everyone's help.

Tell everyone to stand up.... and turn to the right. Then tell them to put their hands on the shoulders of the person in front of you. Now with your fingers, gently start massaging their shoulders.

After a little bit, tell them to give the person some small karate chops on the upper back, then back to the massage.

Then tell everyone to stop and turn the opposite direction and start all over again. This will only take 3 or 4 minutes and it makes everyone feel better and more awake, and it helps everyone to connect.

Chapter Eight

Pick Your Music

Since I am not gifted in playing a musical instrument, singing or leading a group in singing, I rely on the musical talent of others. There have been several times when I have been approached by Scout leaders or Scouts themselves who have offered their musical talent or a favorite CD for musical variety at Chapel Services. If I didn't have a planned CD that tied in with the devotion of the day, I always welcomed their offer. I would tell them of my upcoming devotions and if they or the music in their CD would tie in with it, that would be great. But it wasn't an absolute necessity.

In selecting songs I play at Chapel, I try to keep up with the current popular groups and songs that young people and college students are tuned into. At HSR, I feel comfortable in selecting songs with a Christian intonation. However, if I find that Chapel attendance is going to be of a mixed faith, then I am more selective on the songs I play. If I know something about the artist or the song, I'll tell the scouts what I know. It helps the scouts to relate more to the music, particularly if there is something in common, such as the artist being from the same state or part of the country as they are from.

Music can really add to the devotion or message of the day. Particularly if the words or message of the music can be tied into the devotion. Look for songs that will be an inspiration to your devotion. In some cases I came up with a message that would tie into a song I liked. Point out to your audience how the song ties in to your message.

The following are some of the artists, groups, and songs I have used. Most of the style of music they play is CCM (Contemporary Christian Music), some are Inspirational or P&W (Praise and Worship), and a few are Modern Rock, Pop/Rock, Hip Hop, Christian Rock, and Christian Rap. The lyrics to many of these songs are found at www.songbook.manveladam.com, a Christian Music and Lyric website.

Audio Adrenaline (www.audioa.com)....After 15 years, this Christian Rock group will be performing its final tour in 2006. Lead singer, Mark Stuart started having vocal problems and cannot keep up with a full live performance anymore. His parents were missionaries in Haiti when he was growing up and the group has started, and will continue, to raise awareness and funds for an orphanage in Haiti. The group started out together when they were students at Kentucky Christian College. Their recording "Big House" was awarded the Song of the Decade by CCM Magazine in 1998 and has continued to be a popular song.

BIG HOUSE
Album: Don't Censor Me

I don't know where you lay your head or where you call your home.
I don't know where you eat your meals or where you talk on the phone.
I don't know if you got a cook, a butler, or a maid,
I don't know if you got a yard with a hammock on the shade.

I don't know if you got a shelter, say a place to hide.
I don't know if you live with friends in whom you can confide.
I don't know if you got a family, say a mom or a dad.
I don't know if you feel love at all, but I bet you wish you had.

Come, and go with me, to my Father's house.
Come, and go with me, to my Father's house.
It's a big, big house with lots and lots of room.
A big, big table, with lots and lots of food.
A big, big yard, where we can play football
A big, big house, it's my Father's house.

All I know is a big ole house, with rooms for everyone.
All I know is lots of land, where we can play and run.
All I know is you need love, and I've got a family.
All I know is you're all alone, so why not come with me?

chorus (x4)

Can't Take God Away
Album: Don't Censor Me

You can take God out of the pledge
But you can't take God out of my head

Listen to me closely, lend me your ear
The substance of my statement lets you know I'm sincere
Government officials, shapers of the land
I've got to tell you something you need to understand

You can't take God away from me
You can take my life, my land, my liberty
Lock me up, I'll still be free
'Cause you can't take God from me

You can take God out of the law
You can make me listen to ya'll
You can take God out of the start
But you can't take God out of my heart

Listen to me closely, lend me your ear
The substance of my statement lets you know I'm sincere
Government officials, shapers of the land
I've got to tell you something you need to understand

You can't take God, you can't take God away
repeat (x3)

Big Tent Revival (www.bigtentrevival.net)...This group is based in Memphis, TN and recorded their first album in 1995. They are considered CCM. My favorite song from them is WWJD (What Would Jesus Do).

What Would Jesus Do

Some people just want to survive
And I don't know about you
But I am alive
Lately it seems
That I need a hand
In a fallen world
I just want to stand

What would Jesus do walkin' in my shoes
Workin' at my job and goin' to my school
And I hear people say, "Jesus is the way"
I believe and that is why I'm asking you
What would Jesus do?

And as we all know
Life can be tough
And all that we need is love-sweet love
So where do we go? Well here's what I see
To change my world
I gotta change me

Sometimes choices don't seem black and white
And they can leave you black and blue
(chorus)

WWJD Have you ever thought about it?
What would Jesus do- He'd give his life for you
If you follow Him- you'll give your life to them
What would Jesus do- He'd give his life for you
If you follow Him- you'll give your life to them
Shine on- Shine on- Follow with Jesus

Burlap to Cashmere (www.burlaptocashmere.com)....They started out in 1998 playing Pop/Rock and Folk music in Brooklyn, NY and New Jersey Coffee Houses. Now they also play inspirational music. The song I have used is B.I.B.L.E. (Basic Instructions Before Leaving Earth).

BIBLE

For God so much loved the world
That He gave His one and only son
That whoever believeth in Him
Shall not die but live on

Yes the road is narrow-Yes
The road is tough
But whoever remainth in Him
Shall not die but lift up
Living on through the Son

Steven Curtis Chapman (www.stevencurtischapman.com)....He is known as the King of Christian Music. Starting out in 1987, he was one of the first to introduce Pop/Rock in Christian music. His father had a music store in Paducah, Kentucky and Steven learned to play several types of musical instruments. He has several Grammy's and Gold Albums. He has many songs that can be used, but the two that I have tied in with some of my devotions are 'Saddle Up Your Horses' and 'Dive' (from the album, The Great Adventure).

SADDLE UP YOUR HORSES

Started up this morning in the usual way
Chasing thoughts inside my head of all I had to do today
Another time around the circle
Try and make it better than the last
I opened up the Bible and I read about me
It said I'd been a prisoner and God's grace had set me free
And somewhere between the pages it hit me like a lightning bolt
I saw a big frontier in front of me and I heard somebody say,
"Come on, let's go!"

Saddle up your horses we've got a trail to blaze
Through the wild blue yonder of God's amazing grace
Let's follow our leader into the glorious unknown
This is a life like no other, yeah…this is the Great Adventure!

Come on get ready for the ride of your life
Gonna leave long-faced religion in a cloud of dust behind
And discover all the new horizons just waiting to be explored
This is what we were created for

(chorus)

We'll travel over mountains so high
We'll go through valleys below
Still through it all we'll find that
This is the greatest journey that the human heart will ever see
The love of God will take us far beyond our wildest dreams
Yea…oh saddle up your horses…come on get ready to ride

(chorus)

Chapter Eight

DIVE

The long awaited rains
Have fallen upon the thirsty ground
And carved their way to where the
Wild and rushing rivers can be found
And like the rains
I have been carried here to where the river flows, yeah

My heart is racing and my knees are weak
As I walk to the edge
I know there is no turning back
Once my feet have left the ledge
And in the rush I hear a voice
That's telling me it's time to take the leap of faith
So here I go
I'm diving in, I'm going deep in over my head I want to be
Caught in the rush, lost in the flow
In over my head I want to go
The rivers deep, the rivers wide, the river's water is alive
So sink or swim, I'm diving in

There is a supernatural power
In this mighty rivers flow
It can bring the dead to life
And it can fill an empty soul
And give a heart the only thing
Worth living and worth dying for, yeah
But we will never know the awesome power of the grace of God
Until we let ourselves get swept away
Into this Holy flood
So if you'll take my hand
We'll close our eyes and count to three
And take the leap of faith
Come on let's go

Jars of Clay (www.jarsofclay.com)...This group formed at Illinois Greenville College in 1993. Their music is mostly Christian Pop and Christian Rock. Besides being heard on Christian Radio Stations, you will often hear them on mainstream and modern rock radio. They are now based out of Nashville, TN. One of their songs popular on all rock stations is 'Flood'.

Flood

Rain, rain on my face
It hasn't stopped raining for days
My world is a flood
Slowly I become one with the mud

**But if I can't swim after forty days
And my mind is crushed by the thrashing waves
Lift me up so high that I cannot fall
Lift me up
Lift me up-When I'm falling
Lift me up-I'm weak and I'm dying
Lift me up-I need you to hold me
Lift me up-Keep me from drowning again**

Down on my soul
Splashing in the ocean, I'm losing control
Dark sky all around
I can't feel my feet touching the ground

(chorus)

Calm the storms that drench my eyes
Dry the streams still flowing
Cast down all the waves of sin
And guilt that overthrow me

**(chorus)
(chorus)**

David Crowder (www.davidcrowderband.com).... He is a fairly new artist (national debut was 2002) and is already very popular on the college scene and also one of my personal favorites. He started writing songs while attending Baylor University, a Christian school in Waco, Texas. Crowder and his band helped found the University Baptist Church in Waco in 1996. He realized the music in the local churches was not attracting the college students and he decided to change that. His experimental sounds and use of remixes is exciting and different. I have used several of his songs.

2003 Dove Awards Nominee Song, "Our Love is Loud" off the Album titled, "Can You Hear Us"

OUR LOVE IS LOUD

When we sing
Hear our songs to you
When we dance
Feel us move to you
When we laugh
Fill our smiles with you
When we lift our voices
Louder still
Can you hear us?
Can you feel?

We love you, Lord
We love you
We love you
We love you, Lord
We love you
We love you

When we sing loud
Hear our songs to you

When we dance round
Feel us move to you
When we laugh aloud
Fill our smiles with you
When we lift our voices
Louder still
Can you hear us?
Can you feel?

And our love is big
Our love is loud
Fill this place
(fill our lungs)
With this love now
(to sing it now)

We lift our voices louder still
Our God is near our God is here

You're Everything
Album, "Can You Hear Us"

You're everything
I could want
That I could need
If I could see
You want me
Could I believe
'Cause you're perfectly
All I want
And all I need
If I could just
Feel your touch
Could I be free
Why do you shine so?
Can a blind man see?
Why do you call?
Why do you beckon me?
Can the deaf hear
The voice of love?
Would you have me come?
Can the cripple run?
Are you the one?

To raise me up from this grave
Touch my tongue and then
I'll sing
Heal my limbs then joyfully I'll
Run to you

You're everything
I could want
That I could need
And I can just

Feel your touch
And I can't breathe
Look how you shine so
The blind can see
And how you call
How you beckon me
The deaf hear
The voice of love
You bid me come
And the cripple run
You're the one
Cause you're everything
And I'm alive and I'll sing
And I'm alive and I'm free

EVERY MOVE I MAKE
Album, "The Lime"

Every move I make, I make in You
You made me know Jesus
Every breath I take, I breath in You
Every step I take, I take in You
La, la, la, la………

Waves of Mercy, Waves of Grace
Everywhere I go, I see your Face
Your love has captured me
Oh my God, your Love has captured me
La, la, la, la………

UNDIGNIFIED
Album, "The Lime"

I will dance, I will sing
To be mad for my King
Nothing Lord is hindering
The passion in my soul
And I'll become
Even more undignified than this
Some would say it's foolishness
Leave my pride by the side
But I'll become
Even more undignified than this

DC Talk (www.dctalk.com) ...... Their name gives you a hint where this group is from- Washington D.C. They play CCM, Hip-Hop, Christian Rap, and Pop/Rock. They were the first gospel act to use hip-hop. In 1995, their album "Jesus Freak" sold more copies (over one million) than any other gospel album in history.

CONSUME ME

Lovely traces
I can sense you in everything
The way that you move me
Takes me far away
I seek no escape
I'm dreaming through your eyes
I am wandering through your mind
I'm overtaken
By the way that you delivery me
I'm transcended
There's no place I'd rather be
Than here in heaven
Without you I'm incomplete
It's hopeless

You consume me. You consume me
Like a burning flame running through my veins
You consume me moving through me
Anytime anyplace you invade my space
You consume me. You consume me.

Wholly devoted
I immerse myself in you
Baptize me in your love
'Cause drowning in the thought of you
Floods my soul
I'm taken by the things you do
God you know
It doesn't matter what I lose
I'm yours
(chorus)

Jesus Freak

Separated, I cut myself clean
From a past that comes back in my darkest of dreams
Been apprehended by a spiritual force
And a grace that replaced all the me I've divorced

I saw a man with a tattoo on his big fat belly
It wiggled around like marmalade jelly
It took me a while to catch what it said
Cause I had to match the rhythm of his belly with my head

Jesus Saves is what it raved in a typical tattoo green
He stood on a box in the middle of the city and claimed he had a dream

What will people think when they hear that I'm a Jesus freak
What will people do when they find that it's true
I don't really care if they label me a Jesus freak
Cause there ain't no disguising the truth

Kamikaze my death is gain
I've been marked by my maker a peculiar display
The high and lofty they see me as weak
Cause I won't live and die for the power they seek

There was a man for the desert with maps in his head
The sand that he walked was also his bed
The words that he spoke made the people assume
There wasn't too much left in the upper room
With skins on his back and hair on his face
They thought he was strange by the locusts he ate
The Pharisee's tripped when they heard him speak
Until the King took the head of this Jesus freak

People say I'm strange does it make me a stranger
That my best friend was born in a manger
People say I'm strange does it make me a stranger
That my best friend was born in a manger

What will people think
What will people think
What will people do
What will people do
I don't really care, what else can I say
There ain't no disguising the truth, Jesus is the way

Delirious? (www.delirious.org.uk)….. They formed in 1996 as a worship band for a church in West Sussex, England. It is a few miles south of London. CCM, Christian Rap, and Christian Rock are their music styles. No matter what style of music they are playing, their roots as a worship band still has one thought in mind- to get people connecting with God. They have a slew of great songs.

WITH YOU
Album, "World Service"

Ooh ooh ooh just another day
When being with you shines
A light as I go my way
Ooh ooh ooh just another day
Another moment you and,
I can take it all the way
And its ok cause
I'm with you/ I'm with you, only you
To steal another day
Is all that's on my mind
And I'm staying here to find
That I'm with you
Ooh ooh ooh nothing left to say
When my heart it burns with
Holy fire, don't get in my way
Ooh ooh ooh give it all away
Got to keep these clean hands dirty
If I'm gonna stay awake
But it's okay

You never let me go
You never let me fall
I know you're in this pain
And when I've got it all
And I'm clinging on to you
Cause it's all that we can do
Cause knowing you is beautiful

The Happy Song
Album, "Deeper"

Oh, I could sing unending songs
Of how you saved my soul
Well I could dance a thousand miles
Because of your great love

My heart is bursting Lord
To tell of all you've done
Of how you changed my life
And wiped away the past
I wanna shout it out
From every roof top sing
For now I know that God
Is for me not against me

Everybody's singing now, cause we're so happy
Everybody's dancing now, cause we're so happy
If only we could see your face
And see you smiling over us
And unseen angels celebrate
For joy is in this place

Some other great songs by Delirious on their "Deeper" album…..

SHOUT TO THE NORTH

Men of faith rise up and sing
Of the great and glorious King
You are strong when you feel weak
In your brokenness complete

Shout to the North and the South
Sing to the East and the West
Jesus is savior to all
Lord of heaven and earth

Rise up women of the truth
Stand and sing to broken hearts
Who can know the healing power
Of our awesome King of love

We've been through fire, we've been through rain
We've been refined by the power of His name
We've fallen deeper in love with you
You've burned the truth on our lips

Fill this place with songs again
Of our God who reigns on high
By his grace again we'll fly

I Could Sing Of Your Love Forever

Over the mountains and the sea
Your river runs with love for me
And I will open up my heart
And let the healer set me free
I'm happy to be in the truth
And I will daily lift my hands
For I will always sing
Of when your love came down

I could sing of your love forever (x 4)

Oh I feel like dancing
It's foolishness I know
But when the world has seen the light
They will dance with joy
Like we're dancing now

Did You Feel The Mountains Tremble

Did you feel the mountains tremble?
Did you hear the oceans roar?
When the people rose to sing of
Jesus Christ the risen Lord

Did you feel the people tremble?
Did you hear the singers roar?
When the lost began to sing of
Jesus Christ the saving Lord

And we can see that God you're moving
A mighty river through the nations
And young and old will turn to Jesus
Fling wide you heavenly gates
Prepare the way of the Risen Lord
Open up the doors and
Let the music play
Let the streets resounds with singing
Songs that bring you hope
Songs that bring you joy
Dancers who dance upon injustice
Do you feel the darkness tremble
When all the saints join in one song
And all the streams flow as one river
To wash away our brokenness

And here we see that God you're moving
A time of jubilee is coming
When young and old return to Jesus
Fling wide you heavenly gates
Prepare the way of the risen Lord

I'VE FOUND JESUS

Well I hear they're singing in the street that Jesus is alive
And all creation shouts aloud that Jesus is alive
Now surely we can all be changed cause Jesus is alive
And everybody here can know that Jesus is alive

And I will live for all my days
To raise a hammer of truth and light
To sing about my savior's love
And the best thing that happened
It was the day I met you
I've found Jesus (x 4)

Well I feel like dancing in the street cause Jesus is alive
To join with all who celebrate that Jesus is alive
Well the joy of God is in this town cause Jesus is alive
For everybody's seen the truth that Jesus is alive

(chorus)

Well you lifted me from where I was
Set my feet upon a rock
Humbled that you even knew about me
Now I have chosen to believe
Believing that you've chosen me
I was lost but now I've found....

I'm Not Ashamed

There was a time as a little boy
When I said I'd follow you
But the years have caused the flame
To burn much stronger now
And I'm not burning down any of my bridges
But I'm burning up inside
To flee from my religion and love my neighbor more

I'm not ashamed of the gospel
I'm not ashamed of the one I love
I'm not ashamed of the gospel
I'm not ashamed of the one I love

There were times in my barrenness
When I felt your pure affection
And you heard my frail petitions
To serve you endlessly
But have I loved the tree that they put you on?
Or my friend who met me at the cross?
Oh I want to sing again for my brother
And find my way down this mountain

I'm not ashamed any more
Cause I've felt the oil pour down over me
And there's a fire that's burning stronger now
It's burning stronger much stronger
For you only for you

Darrell Evans (www.darrellevans.com)....... Darrell Evans attended a Bible College in Los Angeles, CA then moved to Tulsa, OK and attended ORU (Oral Roberts University). In Tulsa, he became the worship pastor at Open Bible Fellowship Church and there he recorded his first CCM album. Some of his songs are extemporaneous and may be eight to nine minutes long. The following song lyrics are from his 'Freedom' Album.

So Good To Me

O God you've been so good to me
You came and found this orphan
And you brought me right into your family
O God you've been so good to me
You threw away my past
And you never count my sins against me

You got me dancing
And now I'm shouting
You got me leaping
And now I'm spinning Hallelujah

(Bridge)
You're so good to me
Nah nah nah nah
You're so good to me
Nah nah nah nah

O God you've been so good to me
And every day I wake up
I breathe another breath of your mercy
O God you've been so good to me
And my delight is in you
'Cause I know that your hand is upon me

(repeat chorus)

Jesus you're the one
Who saved myself from me
So I will be the one
To praise you in the streets

Freedom

Where the spirit of the Lord is
There is Freedom
Where the spirit of the Lord is
There is Freedom
There is peace
There is love
There is joy

It is for Freedom you've set us free
It is for Freedom you've set us free

I'm free, I'm free
I'm free, I'm free

(repeat above)

So we will walk in your freedom
Walk in your liberty
We will walk in your freedom
Walk in your liberty

We will dance in your freedom
Dance in your liberty
We will dance in your freedom
Dance in your liberty

Charlie Hall (www.charliehall.com)…..He is one of the regular music worship leaders with 'Passion', the Christian Campus movement for college students all over the world. These students, and young people of this age, number in the tens of thousands. Charlie Hall's home church is Bridgeway Community(www.bridgewaychurch.com) in Oklahoma City with house branches in Norman, Stillwater, and Edmond. His musical style is CCM, Contemporary Folk, and Inspirational.

YOU HAVE DONE GREAT THINGS
From the album, 'Psalm 126'

You have done great things (4x)

When the Lord brought back
The captive ones of Zion
We were like those who dream
Our mouths are filled with laughter
Our tongue with joyful shouting
They say among the nations
The Lord has done great things for them

The Lord has done great things for us (2x)
And we are filled with joy
We are filled with joy

You've restored our hearts
Like streams that flow
Those who sowed in tears
Have reaped their joy
And returned with shouts and songs
Carrying the fruit of God

Sweep Me Away

Prepare the way (2x)
Prepare the way of the Lord
Jesus….

You are the light of the world (3x)
Jesus…

You are the King of the earth (3x)
Jesus…

Shawn McDonald (www.shawnmcdonaldmusic.com)..Another new artist on the scene, here's a CCM artist that has experienced childhood abandonment and substance abuse. He spent a little over four years in China and is now back in the US in Washington State. He finally encountered Christ and now steers others toward Christ.

TAKE MY HAND

Take my hand to the promise land
And on You I want to stand
Cause I cannot do it on my own
You're what I need and I need to be
Right by Your side 'cause I cannot hide
Lord, I know that I need You
Na na na na na na na na na, I need You
Na na na na na nana na na, I need You

Without You I'm so alone
I am weak but You are strong
You pick me up when I'm falling down
And I am crying out to You inside of my heart
I need You, Lord, oh so, for the part
I want You to have my life, Jesus

I fall to my knees
And I'm begging You, please, oh, Lord
Won't You change me
Make me new from the inside out
I want to shout out Your name

Gravity

The ways of this world are grabbing a hold
Won't let me go, won't let me fly by
It's taking its toll down on my soul
Cause I know what I need in my life
Don't let me lose my sight of You
Don't let me lose my sight

I don't want to fall away from You
Gravity is pulling me on down
I don't want to fall away from You
Gravity is pulling me to the ground

This world keeps making me cry
But I'm gonna try, gonna try to fly, gonna fly high
Don't want to give into the sin
Want to stay in You till the end
Don't want to lose my sight of You
Don't want to lose my sight

I want to fly
Into the sky
And turn my back on this old world
And leave it all behind
This place is not my home
It's got nothing for me
Only leaves me with emptiness
And tears in my eyes

Toby Mckeehan (www.tobymac.com)....He's a singer, songwriter and producer who grew up in Washington, DC. There he met fellow DC Talk musicians and formed that band in 1987. Later he formed his own production company (TOBYMAC) and issued his own album in 2001. He combines rock, pop, and rap and his songs are played on both CCM radio stations and regular rock radio stations.

HEY NOW

Hey now, I feel a new one comin' on so that you can sing along with it
Right now and I'm gonna dedicate this song to everyone of God's children
Hey now, one love, one God out of many his people
Right now it's been a long time comin' but I'm serving up the sequel

Back from the day, I'm the sleeper done slumbering
Pass me the mic and I might stop mumbling
Crumble like a cracker, I'll fall like a leaf
But the hole in my soul's been filled underneath
So whether you're a loser or a winner by the numbers
Everyone knows a tie goes to the runner
So lace up your shoes, get yourself in this race
Cause this little thing here gonna set a new pace

Sometimes we do it like this, sometimes we do it like that
Sometimes we say it with words so you can see where we at
And on a different level I persist to reach a girl or any fella
I believe we receive a little then we all do better
Hey now, help is coming anyday now
Hope it can reach me when I am way down
One love, one God and I'm ok now
Ten year, TOBYMAC and GRITS stay down

What you think of this here, gotta get with this here
Diverse City, are you gonna get it this year?
What you think of this here, gotta get with this here
Diverse City and we'll run it till He gets here
Get you back up off the wall
Live a little, come on
Get you back up off the wall
Everybody come on
One love, one God, I feel a new one comin' on so that you can sing along with it
One love, one God, and I'm gonna dedicate this song to everyone of God's children
One love, one God, one love, one God out of many his people
One love, one God, it's been a long time comin' but I'm serving up the sequel
One love, one God

Chapter Eight

ATMOSPHERE

I know you keep a journal and every page is rippled
From the tears that you cry, ain't no meanin' to your scribble
Cause words can't describe what you've been feelin' inside
It's like thousand foot walls, and they're still on the rise
But look up to a beautiful sound
And see for yourself you're not that far down
And know this, I cannot love a little
My promise to you is unconditional
And I'll keep the light on, baby
Just keep the course, you can weather the storm
I'll keep the light on, baby
You've come this far, don't you ever lose heart, now

Just turn around and I'll be there
I'm moving into your atmosphere
Just turn around and I'll be there
I'm moving into your atmosphere

I know you're all alone in a crowd full of friends
I can see it in your eyes that your fadin' again
Checking out, moving into your hole
Where the light can't touch any part of your soul
But hold up and let the river rush in
You can turn around and start livin' again
Cause your life is a beautiful bloom
In the image of the one that created you
I'll be there
Said I'll be there, said I'll be there
Said I'll be there always, forever

Mercy Me (www.mercyme.org)..... Founded in 1994 by the lead singer Bart Millard. He loved playing football with his High School team in Greenville, Texas, but he broke both his ankles so that ended that career. He reluctantly joined the choir in lieu of football. Well, he soon found a gift he didn't know he had. In college, he joined up with a keyboardist and a guitarist and they decided to go full-time into the music ministry. They lived in Orange County for a while and that was where they formed 'Mercy Me'. They moved to Nashville for a time and now they are back in Texas. They play CCM, Inspirational, and Hymns.

I Worship You

I've been walking with a big grin
Singing with my eyes closed
Lifting up my hands
I've been lost in the moment
Sending up praises
Now I think I understand
When I open up and let it flow
I feel your touch and then I know

**I can never live without it
And I'm never going to doubt it
Everyday it's new, yeah
There's nothing any better
I'll be singing it forever
I worship you**

I'm standing on the edge now
Looking to a new place
Going deeper still
The feeling is electric
The power and the glory
Just move me where you will
Cause you take the song and make it fly
Into my soul and that is why

Chorus

I just want to dive into your grace
I want to feel your presence, seek your face
I just want to be where you are
I can never live without it
And I'm never going to doubt it
Everyday is new, yeah

Repeat

Chorus

Here Am I

On the other side of the world
She stands on the ocean shore
gazing at the heavens she wonders
Is there something more
Never been told the name of Jesus
She turns and walks away
What a shame

Just across the street in your hometown
Leaving from his nine to five
Gazing down the road he wonders
Is this all there is to life
Never been told the name of Jesus
He continues on his way
What a shame

Whom shall I send
Who will go for me
To the ends of the earth
Who will rise up for the King
Here am I send me
Here am I send me

Whether foreign land or neighbors
Everyone's the same
Searching for the answers
That lie within your name
I want to proclaim the name of Jesus
In all I do and say
Unashamed

Chorus

How beautiful are the feet of those who bring good news
Proclaiming peace and your salvation

Chris Rice (www.chrisrice.com).... He grew up in Maryland where his parents were owners of a Christian bookstore. Chris started out as a songwriter in the mid-eighties for other artists, and then became a recording artist as well in 1996. He now resides in Nashville, Tennessee. His music is mainly CCM.

CALLING OUT YOUR NAME

Well the moon moved past Nebraska
And spilled laughter on them cold Dakota Hills
And the angels danced on Jacob's stairs
There is this silence in the Badlands
And over Kansas the whole universe was stilled
By the whisper of a prayer
And the single hawk bursts into flight
And in the east the whole horizon is in flames

I feel the thunder in the sky
I see the sky about to rain
And I hear the prairies calling out Your name

I feel the earth tremble beneath
The rumbling of the buffalo hooves
And the fury in the pheasant's wings
It tells me the Lord is in His temple and there is
Still faith that can make the mountains move
And a love that can make the heavens ring
Where the sacred rivers meet beneath
The shadow of the Keeper of the plains

Chorus

From the place where morning gathers
You can look sometimes
Forever 'til you see
What time may never know
How the Lord takes by its corners this old world
To run wild with the hope
The hope that this thirst will not last long
That it will soon drown
In the song not sung in vain

I feel the thunder in the sky
I see the sky about to rain
And with the prairies I am calling out your name

The Cartoon Song

Yea, I was thinking the other day
What if cartoons got saved?
They'd start singing praise
In a whole new way

Fred and Wilma Flintstone sing
Ya-ba-daba-lujah

Scooby-Do and Shaggy
Scooby-do-be-lujay

And the Jetson's dog named Astro
Ra-ra-ru-jah

Chorus

Teenage Mutant Ninja Turtles
Cowabunga-lujay dude

Then there's Kermit the Frog here,
Singing hi-ho-la-lujah

And that little bald guy, Elmer Fudd
Hallelujah, uh

Chorus

Oh that big ol' Moose and his friend Rocky,
Ba-ya-ca-bujah

And our favorite bear named Yogi,
Hi-a-baa-lujah

And there's all those little blue guys
And they'd sing..
La-la-lalalala-lalala-lujah

Oh, how 'bout Beavis and that other guy
Naaaaaah

Chorus

Now there's a point to this looney tune
I'm not an animaniac, but there's a lot of praising to do
And cartoons weren't made for that,
It's our job. Oh, yeah
So let's sing hallelujah (hallelujah)
Hallelujah (hallelujah)
Hallelujah (hallelujah)

Matt Redman (www.mattredman.com)....Matt's music is light and passionate. He is one of the few pop artists who writes his own songs. And he is one of the regular Praise and Worship leaders with Passion. He came on the Christian Contemporary Music charts quickly in 1998 as a thought-provoking songwriter and as a good singer, and he is an inspiration in worship settings all over the world. Matt lives in Watford, England and has a recording studio in Nashville, Tennessee. He holds conferences every year where he is busy training and helping new songwriters and worship leaders of tomorrow.

BETTER IS ONE DAY (PSALM 84:10)

How lovely is your dwelling place
O Lord Almighty
For my soul longs and even faints for you
For here my heart is satisfied
Within your presence
I sing beneath the shadow of your wings

Better is one day in your courts
Better is one day in your house
Better is one day in your courts
Than thousands elsewhere

Repeat

One thing I ask and I would seek
To see your beauty, to find you in the place your glory dwells
My heart and flesh cry out for you, the living God
Your Spirit's water to my soul
I've tasted and I've seen
Come once again to me
I will draw near to you, I will draw near to you

Chorus
Chorus

Let Everything That Has Breath

Let everything that
Everything that
Everything that has breath
Praise the Lord
Repeat (2x)

Praise you in the morning
Praise you in the evening
Praise you when I'm young and when I'm old
Praise you when I'm laughing
Praise you when I'm grieving
Praise you every season of the soul
If we could see how much you're worth
Your power, your might, your endless love
Then surely we would never cease to praise you
Chorus (2x)
Praise you in the heavens
Joining with the angels
Praising you forever and a day
Praise you on the earth now
Joining with creation
Calling all the nations to your praise

Chorus

Michael W. Smith (www.michaelwsmith.com).... Born in West Virginia in 1957, he became a devout Christian 10 years later. He spent his teenage years hanging around other fellow believers who often gathered to play and make music. After high school his support group split up and Michael turned to alcohol and drugs. He had an emotional breakdown in 1979 and as a result he recommitted his life to Christ. As a keyboardist he began recording more rock-oriented Christian music in order to reach a younger audience. As a result he has won both Dove and Grammy Awards and has topped the Billboard charts selling more than seven million records and has had 25 number one hits.

AWESOME GOD

He rolls up His sleeves
He ain't just putting on the ritz
Our God is an awesome God

There is thunder in His footsteps
And lightening in His fists
Our God is an awesome God

The Lord wasn't joking
When He kicked 'em out of Eden
It wasn't for no reason
That He shed His blood
His return is very close
And so you better be believing
That Our God is an awesome God

Our God is an awesome God
He reigns from heaven above
With wisdom, power and love
Our God is an awesome God

And when the sky was starless
In the void of the night
Our God is an awesome God
He spoke into the darkness
And created the light
Our God is an awesome God

Judgement and wrath He poured out on Sodom
Mercy and grace He gave us at the cross
I hope that we have not
Too quickly forgotten that
Our God is an awesome God

Sonic Flood (www.sonicflood.com)…..Nashville, Tennessee based and leaders in the Christian music industry in CCM and Modern Christian Rock. While many Christian bands have gone international, SONICFLOOD has put their emphasis on the growing worship movement in the United States. Christian radio honored them with two Number One Singles ("I Could Sing of Your Love Forever" and "I Want to Know You More").

I WANT TO KNOW YOU MORE

I want to know you more
In the secret, in the quiet place
In the stillness you are there
In the secret, in the quiet hour
I wait only for you
Cause I want to know you more

I want to know you
I want to hear Your voice
I want to know you more
I want to touch you
I want to see your face
I want to know you more

I am reaching for the highest goal
That I might receive the prize
Pressing onward, pushing every
Hinderance aside
Out of my way
Cause, I want to know You more

I Could Sing Of Your Love Forever

Over the mountains and the sea
Your river runs with love for me
And I will open up my heart
And let the Healer set me free
I'm happy to be in the truth
And I will daily lift my hands
For I will always sing
Of when your love came down

I could sing of your love forever
(repeat 3x)

Oh I feel like dancing
It's foolishness I know
But when the world has seen the light
They will dance with joy like we're dancing now

I could sing of your love forever
(repeat 3x)

Ten Shekel Shirt (www.tenshekelshirt.com)…..This group is from New Haven, Connecticut and their music style is Christian Rock, Pop, and Inspirational/ Worship. After a trip to South East Asia in 2002, where they saw case after case of sexually exploited children, they formed JFCI (Justice For Children International) and now raise funds and raise awareness for those children. Two of their top hits are "Meet with Me" and "Ocean" which was on their 2001 debut album "Much".

MEET WITH ME

I'm here to meet with You
Come and meet with me
I'm here to find You
Reveal Yourself to me

As I wait You make me strong
As I long You draw me to Your arms
As I stand and sing Your praise
You come, You come and You fill this place
Won't You come, won't You come
And fill this place

Much

I come to your feet and weep
Remembering how You changed me
I kneel at Your feet humbly
I pour out my love and thanks

I am the one who's been forgiven much
I am the one who loves much

I sit at Your feet in peace
Sensing a smile over me
I'm here at Your feet gladly
Giving my love and my thanks

I am the one who's been
Forgiven much
I am the one who loves much

Chris Tomlin (www.christomlin.com)…. Chris's hometown is Austin, Texas where he co-founded the Austin Stone Community Church. His songs are popular with churches and in Contemporary Services particularly. And as a result millions of churchgoers are singing his songs weekly. Tomlin's CCM and his energy is contagious and charismatic and he easily engages his audience to sing along with him.

GOD OF WONDERS

Lord of all creation
Of water, earth and sky
The heavens are Your tabernacle
Glory to the Lord on High

God of wonders beyond our galaxy
You are holy, holy
The universe declares your majesty
(Precious Lord, reveal Your heart to me)
You are holy, holy

Lord of heaven and earth (2x)

Early in the morning
I will celebrate the light
And as I stumble through the darkness
I will call Your name by night

Hallelujah to the Lord of heaven and earth (3x)

Joyous Light

Hail Gladdening Light, sun so bright
Jesus Christ, end of night, alleluia
Hail Gladdening Light, Eternal Bright
In evening time, 'round us shine, alleluia, alleluia

Hail Gladdening Light, such joyous Light
O Brilliant Star, forever shine, alleluia, alleluia

We hymn the Father, we hymn the Son
We hymn the Spirit, wholly Divine
No one more worthy of songs to be sung
To the Giver of Life all glory is Thine

U2 (www.U2.com)….. This band formed in 1976 is from Dublin, Ireland. With its emphasis on rock and roll, it built a following by 1987 to make it an international superstar band. It has become one of the most popular bands in rock history, with musical styles of Pop/Rock, Post-Punk, and Album Rock. Most of their recordings reach a secular audience but they are also becoming known for their public embracement of Christianity and some of their songs subtly hint of their Christian background. Lead singer, Bono, was the feature speaker for our Nations 54th Annual Prayer Breakfast on Feb.2, 2006. This is a gathering of all cultural faiths and backgrounds whether they be Muslim, Jewish, Buddhist, Hindu, Christian, or others. In an article published by United Christian Broadcasters (www.ucb.co.uk) it states that Bono is a radical believer and follower of Jesus. On the website, www.CCMmagazine.com you can find Bono's remarks made at the National Prayer Breakfast and the interview that followed.

40

I waited patiently for the Lord
He inclined and heard my cry
He brought me up out of the pit
Out of the miry clay

I will sing, sing a new song
I will sing, sing a new song

How long to sing this song?
How long to sing this song?
How long…how long…how long…
How long…to sing this song

He set my feet upon a rock
And made my footsteps firm
Many will see
Many will see and fear

I will sing , sing a new song
I will sing, sing a new song
I will sing, sing a new song
I will sing, sing a new song

How long to sing this song?
How long to sing this song?
How long…how long…how long…
How long…to sing this song

Beautiful Day

The heart is a bloom, shoots up through the stony ground
But there's no room, no space to rent in this town
You're out of luck and the reason that you had to care,
The traffic is stuck, and you're not moving anywhere.
You thought you'd found a friend to take you out of this place
Someone you could lend a hand in return for grace

It's a beautiful day, the sky falls
And you feel like
It's a beautiful day
Don't let it get away

You're on the road but you've got no destination
You're in the mud, in the maze of her imagination
You love this town even if that doesn't ring true
You've been all over
And it's been all over you

It's a beautiful day
Don't let it get away
It's a beautiful day
Don't let it get away

Touch me,
Take me to that other place
Teach me, I know I'm not a hopeless case

See the world in green and blue
See China right in front of you
See the canyons broken by a cloud
See the tuna fleets clearing the sea out
See the Bedouin fires at night
See the oil fields at first light and
See the bird with a leaf in her mouth
After the flood all the colors came out

It was a beautiful
Beautiful day
Don't let it get away

Touch me, take me to that other place
Reach me, I know I'm not a hopeless case

What you don't have you don't need it now
What you don't know you can feel somehow
What you don't have you don't need it now
You don't need it now

Beautiful day
As an angel,
Hit's the ground

4Him (www.4him.net)... This quartet has been voted the Gospel Group of the Year three times. They perform CCM, Holiday, and Contemporary Gospel. In 2005, while sitting down at a McDonald's restaurant in Alabama, they felt God calling them in a new direction. So after 15 years the quartet put together one final Album called 'Encore, For Future Generations'. It is a collection of their career favorites.

Psalm 112

We only get so many times
To ride around this sun
And so many times to see a full moon shine
When day is done
If anything's worth doing
Then it's worth doing right
So I looked for wisdom on how to
Best live this brief life I have found

Blessed is he who fears the Lord
Who finds delight in His commands
Blessed is he who fears the Lord
Who finds delight in His Commands

I guess that we all gamble on some
Truth to guide our days
And we trust that it will bring us joy and meaning on the way
I've got friends who feel betrayed by all the things
They once believed
So with everything I've seen I've gotta say it seems to me

Chorus
Please hear this from a humble heart
But I feel like "exhibit A"
In the evidence that God is good to those
Who live by faith, that's why I believe

Chorus
He will not be shaken
He will have no fear
He will then remember

The Only Thing I Need

Eyes closed in a veil of tears when I hear the sound
Once more you've come to me- You've calmed me down
You still the raging sea inside of me
My Lord has come to me

Why is it so hard for me to see
Why is it so hard to just believe
Show me what it means to be free

The only thing I need I already have
The fullness of your mercy in my hand

The only one who loves me as I am
The only thing I need I already have

My heart- a companion to my wounded soul
Again you comfort me… you take control
You quell the fear that owns too much of me
As it was meant to be

So why…when each and every word becomes a war
When there's nothing I can see worth fighting for
You came into my heart and set me free

You're all I need…already have it
All I need…already have it
All in need…already have it

Conclusion

In the interview with U2's Bono, after his talk at the 2006 National Prayer Breakfast, he commented:

"There's something going on... a movement...with heat. In the past, the church has been behind on some issues, but the church hasn't missed this time- it is leading. This is amazing to me." He went on to say, ten years ago he couldn't have believed this would or could ever happen. It's still hard for him to believe it's really happening.

U2 is popular all over the world and has a large secular following. Their music is popular on secular radio stations and rarely heard on Christian Radio Stations.

Now hear about an interview with Matt Redman whose music is popular around the world and has a strictly Christian following. His music is popular in churches and on Christian Radio Stations and he is probably never heard on secular radio stations. Matt's interview on www.worshiptogether.com about the movement going on today with Passion and other similar groups. "There's something so exciting about seeing a movement that God has raised up. When it's something no one tried to make happen or manufacture....It's quite a humbling and inspiring thing to go to an event like Passion One Day and see tens of thousands of young people (from all over the world) crying out to God...."

I agree that God is stirring things up right now. Why, I'm not sure. Maybe it's a combination of things...but this movement is alive and growing. Perhaps 300 to 500 years from now theologians will be able to point to the reason why God raised up this movement at this time. Perhaps it will be called "The 2nd Millennium Movement", the movement that began 2000 years after the birth of Jesus Christ.

I hope that this book may be an encouragement to others to get involved in the movement and to lead young men and women of today to a closer relationship with God.

And lastly this thought from the book of Jeremiah, Jeremiah urges everyone who is hard of heart or who has closed ears to heed his words and to turn to God and receive His love and His message of eternal life with Him. Jeremiah's message reminds me of the words spoken by a wise and thoughtful man who was asked if he believed if there was a Heaven and a Hell. He replied that he would rather believe there is a Heaven and be wrong, than not to believe and find out, too late, that he was wrong.

ISBN 141209310-4